City Cuisine

City Cuisine ✕

Mary Sue Milliken

Susan Feniger

written with Helene Siegel

photographs by Michael Fink

Hearst Books / New York

M.S.M. dedicates her efforts in these pages to R.M., J.M., and C.D.

It is the policy of William Morrow and Company, Inc., and its imprints and affiliates, recognizing the importance of preserving what has been written, to print the books we publish on acid-free paper, and we exert our best efforts to that end.

Library of Congress Cataloging-in-Publication Data

Milliken, Mary Sue
    City cuisine/Mary Sue Milliken and Susan Feniger; written with Helene Siegel.
        p.   cm.
    Includes index.
    ISBN 0-688-13177-8
    1. Cookery.   I. Feniger, Susan.   II. Milliken, Mary Sue.
III. Title.
TX714.F46   1989
641.5—dc 19   88-21551
                                                        CIP

Printed in the United States of America

First Hearst Paperback Edition 1994

1 2 3 4 5 6 7 8 9 10

Contents

Acknowledgments

City Cuisine is the product of a strong partnership, tempered by the constant input of new and creative experiences. We wish to acknowledge directly some of the people who strongly influence us, past, present, and future. Jovan Treboyevic, Gus Reidi, Wolfgang Puck, Gregory Duda, Patrick Terrail, and Alan Wagner have provided the wisdom and talent of great mentors. Our enthusiastic staff inspires us daily with a burning energy that feeds our creative fires. We thank our mothers, Ruth and Ruthie, who taught us to appreciate fine food from the start. But how to thank those who awoke in us a love for cooking in its most essential and cultural forms—from the Indian women who cooked naan for five hundred to the many international vendors whose "street foods" are the basis of many of our recipes?

Introduction

City Cuisine is food that speaks to you with assertive flavors, textures, and colors. It is the result of a partnership, not only between two dedicated chefs, but between two worlds of cuisine. After ten years of rigorous training in French kitchens, our sensibilities were shocked by visits to India, Mexico, Thailand, and Japan. We saw food being transformed from its most essential and primitive forms into country dishes with spirit and heart. The science and technique of food preparation that we had been trained to follow was augmented with a cultural cooking tradition that demanded attention for its uniqueness and quality.

In reading *City Cuisine,* you will notice the counterbalance of these varied styles of cooking. We've taken the best of ethnic foods, brought some to a more refined level, and left others in their original form. The disciplinary rules of haute cuisine are bent without losing quality, and we've added flexibility and richness to our recipes. We follow five main points when cooking, and list them here to help guide you into our culinary perspective.

The Flavor We are drawn to strong, bold flavors and exotic seasonings. Remember, this food is direct and forceful, not subtle.

The Taste During the process of cooking these recipes, your best tool is your tongue. Taste, adjust, taste again, readjust, and most important, trust what you like. If there is a single key to our success with food, it is this.

The Look A combination of textures, shapes, heights, and colors makes a plate appealing. Focus on the main ingredient, keeping it simple, yet sophisticated. Make the food precise, not overly handled.

The Ingredients Inspirational moments begin for us during visits to various markets. Try Asian fish markets, ethnic groceries, simple roadside stands, or your own organic gardens.

Health Through the use of powerful seasonings we have been able to reduce our dependency on creams, butters, and oils. We also incorporate many basic, healthful ethnic ingredients into our everyday cooking.

1 Starters

Spicy Starters

Small portions are just the right place to begin experimenting with spicy flavors and exotic combinations. Our goal in these personal favorites from India and Thailand is to balance spicy flavors with sweet and salty.

Blending spices is truly an interpretive art. Please adjust the amounts of chiles, Tabasco, and cayenne in these recipes to suit your and your guests' tastes. Simply start with less than the amount called for, then taste, and adjust, if necessary.

We prefer the smaller and hotter serranos to jalapeño chile peppers. Once again, this is purely personal. If you want less heat, just use a larger chile or remove the seeds. Always wash your hands after handling chile peppers to remove the hot oils.

Fried Fish Fingers with Honey-Mustard Dipping Sauce

*Beer is the secret to this
exceptionally light
batter-fried fish. The
yeast from the beer
causes the batter to rise
and expand.*

6 servings

1 cup all-purpose flour

2 teaspoons cayenne pepper

2 teaspoons salt

½ teaspoon baking powder

1 teaspoon granulated sugar

1 (8-ounce) bottle of beer, room temperature

1½ pounds skinless halibut, sole, or flounder fillets

4 cups peanut oil for frying

lemon wedges for garnish

Honey-Mustard Dipping Sauce, recipe follows

Combine flour, cayenne, salt, baking powder, and sugar in a medium bowl. Add beer, all at once, and whisk until smooth. Set aside, uncovered, at least an hour.

Slice fish into ¼ × 2-inch strips.

Heat oil to deep-fry temperature (350°F) in a large saucepan. Test oil by sprinkling in a few drops of batter. If they immediately rise to the surface, the oil is ready. Thoroughly coat strips by dipping one at a time in batter. Fry 4 or 5 pieces at a time until crisp and golden, about 2 minutes. Remove with a slotted spoon and drain on paper towels. Serve immediately with lemon wedges and Honey-Mustard Dipping Sauce.

Honey-Mustard Dipping Sauce

6 tablespoons honey

¼ cup Dijon mustard

15 to 30 dashes of Tabasco

Mix ingredients together in a small bowl.

makes ¾ cup

Vegetable Fritters with Chick-Pea Batter and Two Sauces

These spicy fritters are a popular late afternoon snack with a cool glass of Lemon Ginger Tea (page 229). Almost any vegetable can be substituted for those listed—cabbage and onion are popular in India, where Susan learned this recipe.

6 servings

1 cup fine chick-pea flour (page 233)
1 tablespoon ground cumin
1 tablespoon black mustard seeds (page 232)
1 teaspoon salt
1 teaspoon dried red pepper flakes
½ teaspoon turmeric
½ teaspoon cayenne pepper
½ teaspoon cornstarch
¼ teaspoon ground coriander
¼ teaspoon baking powder
¾ to 1 cup water
1 teaspoon peanut or vegetable oil
6 cups vegetable oil for frying
1 bell pepper, cored, seeded, and sliced in ½-inch strips
6 medium mushrooms, whole or sliced in half
1 cup broccoli florets
2 cups cauliflowerets
Mint and Cilantro Chutney, recipe follows
Yogurt Sauce, recipe follows

Mix flour and dry ingredients together in a large bowl. Add ¾ cup water and stir to combine. Gradually add more water until mixture is thick enough to coat a finger. Stir in peanut oil. The batter may be made up to 2 hours in advance.

To make fritters, heat oil in a large saucepan to deep-fry temperature (350°F). Dip vegetables, one at a time, in batter to evenly coat. Fry, a few at a time, until deep brown, about 2 minutes. Remove with a slotted spoon and drain on paper towels. Serve immediately with Mint and Cilantro Chutney, Yogurt Sauce, and soy sauce for dipping.

Mint and Cilantro Chutney

3 bunches cilantro, stems trimmed and finely chopped

1 small bunch fresh mint, leaves only, finely chopped

2 garlic cloves, minced

1½ tablespoons freshly grated ginger (page 235)

1 to 2 serrano chiles, finely chopped with seeds

½ teaspoon salt

juice of 1 small lemon

½ tablespoon peanut oil

makes 1¾ cups

Mix ingredients in a bowl. Turn out onto a board and chop until a paste is formed.

Yogurt Sauce

3 tablespoons peanut oil

2 teaspoons black (page 232) or yellow mustard seeds

2 teaspoons cumin seeds

2 teaspoons pureed garlic (page 236)

1 teaspoon freshly grated ginger (page 235)

½ teaspoon turmeric

½ teaspoon paprika

⅛ teaspoon dried red pepper flakes

½ teaspoon salt

1 pint plain yogurt

With ingredients measured and nearby, heat oil in a small skillet over high heat. Add mustard seeds. Cover immediately and cook until popping stops.

Lower heat, add cumin seeds, and cook until they turn golden, about 1 minute. Stir in garlic for 10 seconds, then ginger for 10 seconds more, and remove from heat. Stir in turmeric, paprika, pepper flakes, and salt. Mix spices and yogurt in a bowl. Chill before serving.

makes 2 cups

Fried Clams with Homemade Tartar and Spicy Cocktail Sauces

Great fried clams are surprisingly easy to prepare at home. In this dish, the spice is in the sauce, so your guests can indulge their hot tooth accordingly. We have found Ipswich clams to be extraordinary for this dish, though littlenecks can be good also.

6 servings

4 dozen clams, freshly shucked, or 1 pound shucked
4 eggs
1½ cups all-purpose flour
1½ cups fine dry bread crumbs
6 cups vegetable oil for frying
lime wedges for garnish
Homemade Tartar Sauce, recipe follows
Spicy Cocktail Sauce, recipe follows

Pat clams dry and reserve. Beat eggs in a medium bowl and place flour and bread crumbs in individual bowls. Dip clams, 3 to 4 at a time, in flour, patting off any excess. Then dip in eggs and bread crumbs. Set aside on a platter.

Heat oil to deep-fry temperature (350°F) in a large saucepan. Add clams, a handful at a time, being careful of spattering oil. Do not overcrowd pan or oil will become too cool. Fry until golden brown all over, about 1 minute, taking care not to overcook. Remove with a slotted spoon and drain on paper towels. Serve immediately with lime wedges, Homemade Tartar Sauce, and Spicy Cocktail Sauce.

Homemade Tartar Sauce

¾ cup Mayonnaise (page 179)
1 tablespoon fresh lemon juice
2 tablespoons dill pickle finely chopped
2 tablespoons finely chopped red onion
2 tablespoons finely chopped capers
2 tablespoons finely chopped celery
2 tablespoons finely chopped parsley leaves
½ teaspoon salt
½ teaspoon freshly ground black pepper
1 tablespoon stone-ground mustard

makes 1 cup

Mix ingredients together in a bowl.

Spicy Cocktail Sauce

¾ cup ketchup
1 to 2 serrano chiles, finely chopped with seeds
3 tablespoons chopped fresh cilantro leaves
3 tablespoons finely chopped red onion
1½ tablespoons fresh lime juice
½ teaspoon salt
½ teaspoon freshly ground black pepper
Tabasco to taste

makes 1 cup

Mix ingredients together in a bowl.

Thai Melon Salad

This authentic Thai dressing, packed with savory ingredients like garlic, chiles, peanuts, and dried shrimp, accentuates the coolness of summer melons. The dish looks lovely prepared with alternating rows of brightly colored melons: We like to use cantaloupe, watermelon, crenshaw, and honeydew.

6 servings

3 garlic cloves, pureed (page 236)

2 tablespoons palm sugar (page 234) or brown sugar

¼ cup Thai Fish Sauce (page 235)

¼ cup fresh lime juice

3 or more serrano chiles to taste, stems removed and thinly sliced with seeds

1 tablespoon chopped kaffir lime leaves (page 234) or 1 teaspoon grated lime zest

½ cup dried shrimp (page 233)

½ cup roasted, unsalted peanuts

6 cups assorted melon cubes, in ½-inch cubes, each variety separated

¼ cup fresh cilantro leaves for garnish

Mix garlic, palm or brown sugar, Thai Fish Sauce, lime juice, chiles, and lime leaves in a medium bowl. Roughly chop shrimp and peanuts by hand or in a food processor and add to garlic mixture. (The dressing can be made in advance and stored up to 3 days in the refrigerator.)

To serve, arrange each variety of melon cubes in alternating rows on a platter or in individual bowls. Spoon dressing over melon in a stripe and garnish with cilantro. Serve chilled.

Chinese Sausage Salad

This sweet and spicy dish was part of an elaborate midday buffet Mary Sue prepared during her first trip to Thailand. The festive salad is served in hollow red onion cups—a typical Thai presentation.

6 servings

1 (12-ounce) package sweet Chinese sausage (page 233)
2 medium red onions, wide around the middle
5 pickling cucumbers or Kirbies (page 234), with skins
inner leaves from 1 bunch celery, washed and roughly chopped
1 bunch cilantro, leaves only
4 to 6 serrano chiles, stems removed and thinly sliced, diagonally
1 tablespoon chopped kaffir lime leaves (page 234) or 1 teaspoon
 grated lime zest
2 teaspoons pureed garlic (page 236)
¼ cup palm sugar (page 234) or brown sugar
½ cup fresh lime juice
½ cup Thai Fish Sauce (page 235)

Preheat broiler. Place sausages in one layer on a large baking sheet and broil until charred on all sides, about 5 minutes per side. Set aside to cool.

To make onion cups, slice off root ends and tops, then peel. Cut each in half horizontally, and separate layers by pressing with your thumbs against root end to release rings. Reserve 12 largest as serving cups. Slice remaining onion into thin strips for use in salad.

Slice cucumbers in half lengthwise. Then thinly slice cucumbers and charred sausages, diagonally.

Combine sausage, cucumbers, onion strips, celery leaves, and cilantro in a medium bowl. In another bowl, whisk together serrano chiles, lime leaves, garlic, palm or brown sugar, lime juice, and Thai Fish Sauce. Pour over salad and toss to combine.

To serve, place onion cups open-side up on each serving plate. Spoon salad into cups and serve.

Poona Pancakes

These crisp and savory
pancakes, named for
the city in India where
Susan first tasted them,
are a pleasant surprise
to American taste buds.
In India they are served
topped with a fried egg
for breakfast, quite a
contrast to our sweet
breakfast cakes.

8 servings or 64
canapés

1 cup basmati rice (page 232)
1 cup black bean dal (page 233) or lentils
3 cups water
5 tablespoons plain yogurt
1½ teaspoons salt
2 tomatoes, peeled, seeded, and diced (page 236)
2 serrano chiles, stems and seeds removed, diced
1 small red onion, diced
½ bunch cilantro, stems trimmed, roughly chopped
⅓ cup vegetable oil
yogurt, chopped tomatoes, and chopped cilantro for garnish

Pick over rice and dal to remove any pebbles or dirt. Process in a food processor or blender until a coarse flour, about 5 minutes.

Mix ground mixture with water, yogurt, and salt in a bowl. Cover with plastic wrap and set aside in a warm place at least 12 hours or as long as 24. When ready, batter should be smooth and foamy, a bit thinner than pancake batter.

Just before cooking, add tomatoes, serrano chiles, red onion, and cilantro. Stir to combine.

Heat 1 tablespoon oil in a small, well-seasoned cast-iron skillet over high heat until very hot. Pour in ⅓ cup batter, reduce heat to low, and spread batter evenly with a ladle or spatula. Fry until well browned, about 2 to 3 minutes per side. Repeat this procedure, heating an additional tablespoon oil each time, until all batter is fried.

Stack pancakes between layers of aluminum foil in a roasting pan and keep warm in a 200°F oven. To serve, arrange 2 pancakes on each plate and top with yogurt, tomatoes, and cilantro. For smaller servings, slice each pancake into quarters and serve with garnishes for dipping.

Marinated Fish and Meats

Marinated foods are great for hot weather entertaining. All are easy to prepare, low in calories, and taste best served icy cold.

It is essential to use the freshest meat and fish for these simple dishes. If you live in the middle of the country, the availability of fresh food has vastly improved: Special airfreight companies are shipping Louisiana crayfish, Maine lobsters, and fish from both coasts, South America, Hawaii, and Europe daily to the Midwest. If you live along the coast, it's worth a trip to the local fish market, where the restaurant buyers shop.

Oysters on the Half Shell with Red Wine Vinegar Sauce

Red wine vinegar and shallots, pureed in a blender, give oysters a more delicate, festive feeling than the usual sharp cocktail sauce. To serve the oysters extra cold, line the plates with crushed ice and sprinkle with Kosher salt. Then arrange oysters on the ice shell-side down, garnished with seaweed in the center.

6 servings

6 shallots, peeled and sliced
¾ cup red wine vinegar
36 fresh oysters

Puree shallots and red wine vinegar in a blender until smooth. Set aside. (Do not make this simple sauce far in advance or the delicate flavors will fade.)

To shuck oysters, wash under cold, running water and scrub with a stiff brush to remove any surface sand, especially around seam. With a towel in the palm of your hand to protect it, press shell against a work counter. In the pointy end of the oyster insert tip of oyster knife, gently twist to break seal, and run knife around edges until shell opens. Discard empty top shells. Dab around oyster with tip of wet towel to remove any bits of broken shell or sand. You can further clean, if necessary, with a pastry brush dipped in icy salted water. Shucked oysters may be kept, covered with a wet towel, in the refrigerator up to an hour.

Loosen the muscle that holds the oyster to the shell by gently sliding a knife between the two. Arrange 6 oysters per serving on chilled plates. Spoon about 1 teaspoon sauce over each oyster to cover with a thin layer. Serve immediately.

Marinated Tuna with Spiced Sprouts

*These thin slices
of tuna must be
marinated very briefly
to maintain the finest
texture and taste. You
can prepare bite-sized
rolls by cutting small
rectangular slices and
wrapping each around
a small bouquet of
sprouts. With either
presentation, spoon on
the marinade just
before serving.*

4 servings

1 pound skinless, boneless tuna, such as Hawaiian yellow fin
½ cup brown rice vinegar (page 232) or rice wine vinegar (page 234)
2½ tablespoons soy sauce
2 tablespoons mirin (page 234)
2 tablespoons freshly grated ginger (page 235)
2 (2-ounce) packages daikon spiced sprouts (page 233), roots
   trimmed
½ medium red onion, shredded

Using a sharp, wet knife, thinly slice tuna along grain using a long, horizontal sawing motion. The easiest way to do this is to press the fish down with one hand and cut slices off the top. Cover four serving plates with tuna. The lined plates may be reserved in refrigerator, covered with plastic wrap, up to 4 hours.

Mix vinegar, soy sauce, mirin, and ginger in a small bowl and spread about 2 tablespoons over each serving, evenly coating fish. Divide sprouts and arrange in a small fan on the side of each plate. Divide the red onion and place a small mound at root end of sprouts. Spoon a bit of dressing over sprouts and serve immediately.

Beef Carpaccio

Avoid the temptation to release your frustrations when pounding raw beef. The best carpaccio is the result of gentle flattening rather than aggressive pounding, which breaks down the fibers and dulls the taste.

Use the freshest beef, of course. Susan, a raw-beef fanatic, suggests serving carpaccio before an entrée of Rigatoni Stuffed with Chicken and Fennel (page 92) or Roasted Black Cod with Coulis of Horseradish (page 105).

8 servings

1 pound beef sirloin, trimmed of all fat and sinew
¾ cup olive oil
juice of 1 lemon
8 large shallots, finely diced
1 teaspoon salt
1 tablespoon plus 1 teaspoon cracked black peppercorns (page 235)
julienned Parmesan cheese and chopped fresh chives for garnish

Chill 8 serving plates. Place meat in freezer about 10 minutes.

Whisk together olive oil, lemon juice, shallots, salt, and pepper in a small bowl and reserve.

Slice cold beef across grain into ⅛-inch slices. Then place each slice, one at a time, between 2 sheets plastic wrap and, using the smooth side of a meat pounder, flatten by gently pounding and pressing back and forth. Work from center out. Keep turning to flatten it evenly to about 1/16 inch. (You should spend about a minute on each slice.)

Entirely cover each chilled plate with thin slices beef. (At this stage, you can cover with plastic wrap and reserve in refrigerator for several hours.) Carefully spoon reserved dressing over meat to evenly cover. Garnish with Parmesan strips and chives, and serve immediately.

Fish Tartare

Here is a pretty dish combining the chunky texture and strong tastes of beef tartare with delicately flavored fish. Feel free to substitute according to availability and freshness. Tuna or scallops could replace the salmon, and any mild fish, such as red snapper or sole, could stand in for the halibut.

4 servings

8 ounces skinless, boneless salmon

8 ounces skinless, boneless halibut

juice of 2 limes

1 egg yolk

1 tablespoon Dijon mustard

1 teaspoon salt

½ teaspoon freshly ground black pepper

½ cup extra virgin olive oil

2 dashes of Tabasco

12 cornichons, finely diced

6 shallots, finely diced

⅓ cup capers, drained and chopped

3 tablespoons chopped fresh parsley leaves

3 tablespoons chopped fresh chives

red leaf lettuce for garnish

Using a sharp, wet knife, cut fish into ¼-inch cubes. Combine fish and lime juice in a glass or ceramic bowl. Cover with plastic wrap and refrigerate a minimum of 5 minutes or as long as 15 minutes.

Whisk egg yolk, mustard, salt, and pepper together in a mixing bowl. Gradually add olive oil, whisking constantly, until mayonnaise is formed. (You can thin the mixture with a few drops of lime juice, if necessary.) Stir in Tabasco, cornichons, shallots, capers, parsley, and chives.

Drain fish in a colander. Combine with mayonnaise and toss to evenly coat. To serve, line plates with lettuce leaves. Top with a scoop of fish tartare and serve immediately with toasted French bread or crackers.

Gravlax with Dill Mayonnaise

4 to 6 servings

2 tablespoons whole coriander seeds
¼ cup coarse salt
¼ cup cracked black peppercorns (page 235)
⅓ cup granulated sugar
2 pounds skinless salmon fillet
1 bunch dill
Dill Mayonnaise, recipe follows

Cook coriander seeds in a small dry sauté pan over moderate heat just until the aroma is released. Crush seeds using the bottom of a heavy pot or a mortar and pestle. Mix seeds with salt, pepper, and sugar in a small bowl and reserve.

Slice salmon in half across width and lay pieces side by side on counter, flesh-side up. Divide dry spice mixture in half and sprinkle one half over both pieces. Place half the dill sprigs on 1 piece salmon and top with remaining piece salmon to enclose the spices and herbs, as if making a sandwich. (Make the sandwich even by placing the thick end of salmon on top of thin end.)

Evenly coat outside of salmon sandwich with remaining spices and dill. Tightly wrap in 2 layers plastic wrap, place in a shallow baking dish, and top with weights (canned goods or milk cartons are good). Refrigerate 3 days, turning over every 12 hours.

To serve, scrape off spices and dill. Slice thinly and serve cold with Dill Mayonnaise and thinly sliced black bread.

Dill Mayonnaise

4 egg yolks
1 tablespoon Dijon mustard
3 tablespoons tarragon vinegar
1 tablespoon granulated sugar
1¼ cups olive oil
¾ cup soybean oil
1 bunch chopped fresh dill leaves
½ teaspoon salt
½ teaspoon freshly ground black pepper

In a bowl, combine egg yolks, mustard, vinegar, and sugar. Blend with whisk. Gradually add olive oil and soybean oil, a drop at a time, whisking constantly. As mayonnaise begins to thicken, add oils more generously. Whisk in dill, salt, and pepper. Adjust seasonings and store in refrigerator up to 24 days.

makes 2 cups

Lamb's Tongue with Thyme Vinaigrette

When visualizing this dish, forget about large boiled beef tongues. Lamb's tongues, available at most butcher shops, are tiny. In this refreshing salad, they're sliced thinly and then tossed with a pungent vinaigrette— great warm weather food!

4 to 6 servings

9 lamb's tongues

2 bay leaves

1 bunch fresh thyme, leaves and stems separated

2 tablespoons black peppercorns

1 teaspoon salt

2 shallots, finely diced

⅓ cup extra virgin olive oil

juice of 1 small lemon

salt and freshly ground black pepper to taste

red leaf lettuce for garnish

Combine tongues, bay leaves, thyme stems, peppercorns, and salt in a large stockpot with about 1 gallon of water. Bring to a boil and reduce to a simmer. Cook, uncovered, until tongues easily slide off when pierced with a fork, about 1½ hours. Remove from heat. Reserve tongues in cooking liquid.

Peel tongues by dipping, one at a time, in a bowl of iced water. Immediately remove any skin or tough gristle with your fingers or a small paring knife. Place in a bowl, cover with plastic wrap, chill for 1 hour.

To make the vinaigrette, combine shallots, oil, and lemon juice with half the chopped thyme leaves in a small bowl. Whisk thoroughly and season with salt, pepper, and additional thyme, to taste.

When properly chilled, slice tongues thinly across the grain. Toss with vinaigrette. Arrange a bed of lettuce leaves on each plate. Place a scoop of tongue vinaigrette in center of each and serve.

Variation: Broiled clams are delicious with thyme vinaigrette. Arrange open clams on the half shell on a baking sheet, open-side up. Spoon about 1 teaspoon thyme vinaigrette over each to completely cover. Broil about 2 minutes and serve hot.

Marinated Scallops and Watercress Salad

1 pound sea scallops

MARINADE
½ cup extra virgin olive oil
juice of 2 limes
6 shallots, finely diced
2 small bunches cilantro, leaves only, coarsely chopped
1¼ teaspoons salt
¼ teaspoon freshly ground black pepper

1 recipe Watercress and Avocado Salad (page 165)

Carefully clean scallops of any roe, muscle, or brown connective tissue, which can become tough when marinated. Cut scallops into ¼-inch horizontal slices.

Combine marinade ingredients in a small bowl. Add scallops and toss to coat. Marinate, covered, in refrigerator 5 minutes or as long as ½ hour. (Any longer and the acid in the lime juice would overcook the seafood.)

Meanwhile prepare Watercress and Avocado Salad, reserving avocados.

To serve, divide dressed watercress salad among 6 serving plates. Arrange a circle of scallops in center of each and garnish with avocado slices along the side. Spoon leftover marinade over scallops and avocado. Serve cold.

It doesn't take the skill of a sushi chef to prepare this luxurious scallop salad. We prefer large sea scallops, which are easy to slice with any sharp knife, and their buttery consistency is enhanced by only a brief marinade.

6 servings

Vegetarian Appetizers

Our small vegetarian plates fulfill many needs. With the exception of the Avocado Grapefruit Salad (page 30), which is strictly a starter, all the dishes can be served as hearty appetizers or light main courses for lunch or dinner. All they need is a simple green salad and some bread to make a complete meal.

Cheese gives these dishes heartiness. We like to use strong, salty cheeses like feta, Parmesan, and goat cheese, almost as you would spices, to add body and flavor to milder foods.

Glazed Eggplant

A special harmony exists in the earthy combination of eggplant, tomatoes, and Parmesan cheese. Although this recipe seems long, the Tomato Concassé (page 29), Hollandaise, and eggplant can all be made up to 3 hours in advance. This hearty appetizer is a good way to begin a dinner of your favorite roasted meat.

6 servings

HOLLANDAISE

3 egg yolks
1 tablespoon water
2 teaspoons fresh lemon juice
⅛ teaspoon salt
⅛ teaspoon freshly ground black pepper
¾ cup clarified butter (page 235), warm

In a medium bowl over simmering water, vigorously whisk together egg yolks, water, lemon juice, salt, and pepper until mixture is thick and fluffy, 3 to 5 minutes. The yolks should leave a trail when you lift the whisk. Remove from heat.

Gradually add clarified butter, a few drops at a time, whisking constantly. After half has been incorporated, you can add larger amounts of butter. Reserve up to 3 hours in a warm place.

1 cup olive oil for frying
1 medium eggplant, with skin, cut in ½-inch horizontal (round) slices
¾ cup Tomato Concassé (page 29), warm
½ cup heavy cream
½ cup freshly grated Parmesan cheese

Preheat broiler.

Heat oil in a medium skillet over moderate heat. Sauté eggplant until lightly golden, 1 to 2 minutes per side. Drain on paper towels and arrange in 1 layer on a baking sheet or individually on the ovenproof plates it's to be served on. Spread about 2 tablespoons Tomato Concassé over each slice and reserve.

(continued)

Whip cream until soft peaks form. Gently fold cream and Parmesan cheese into reserved Hollandaise. Spoon over Tomato Concassé, to cover each slice. Broil until golden and bubbly, about 2 minutes. Serve immediately.

Roasted Red Peppers with Feta

This easy appetizer contrasts sweet, meaty red peppers with tangy feta. Look for Bulgarian feta in your local cheese shop or ethnic delicatessan. It's softer and less salty than the Greek type.

12 servings

12 ounces feta cheese, preferably Bulgarian (page 232), room
    temperature
1 cup olive oil
6 large red bell peppers
24 basil leaves
½ cup extra virgin olive oil

Drain feta of any water. Crumble into a small bowl and marinate in olive oil, at room temperature, until peppers are ready.

Char peppers on all sides under a preheated broiler or directly over a gas flame. Transfer to a plastic bag, close tightly, and set aside to steam, about 10 minutes. Under cold running water, carefully peel and split peppers open to remove seeds and excess pulp. Cut each into 4 equal pieces.

On each of 12 salad plates or a large platter, place 12 smaller pieces of pepper, skinned-side down. Cover each with a basil leaf and spread with 1 heaping tablespoon feta. Cover with another basil leaf and top with a larger piece of pepper. Drizzle 1 teaspoon extra virgin olive oil over each and serve at room temperature.

Variation: For finger food, cut peppers into smaller pieces and roll with basil and feta into bite-sized roll-ups. At Christmastime we like to arrange platters of alternating red, green, and yellow peppers.

Goat Cheese Avocado

Marinated goat cheese adds just the right kick to the soothing taste and texture of avocado in this simple spread. We never grow tired of eating it—as an appetizer, on French bread sandwiches, or with chips and crackers, as a dip. We suggest you keep a stash in the refrigerator for summer snacks. Inspired by partner Barbara, this snack became a staple at Susan's house.

6 servings

4 ounces mild, soft goat cheese such as Montrachet
½ cup olive oil
4 ripe avocados, halved, seeded, and peeled
juice of 1 lemon
4 dashes Tabasco
⅛ teaspoon freshly ground black pepper
salt to taste
tomato wedges, cucumber slices, and thin rounds of French bread
    for garnish

Marinate goat cheese in olive oil, in a small covered container, at room temperature, at least a day. (You can add fresh herbs and spices such as basil, thyme, rosemary, and peppercorns, if you wish, to flavor cheese.) Goat cheese can marinate indefinitely, as long as completely covered with oil.

Before serving, lift cheese out of oil. Combine with avocados, lemon juice, Tabasco, and pepper in a large bowl. Mash with a fork until mixture is slightly lumpy, *not* a smooth puree. Season sparingly with salt, since goat cheese can be very salty.

To serve, center a scoop on small salad plates. Garnish with tomato wedges, thick cucumber slices, and thin rounds of French bread.

Variation: This is a great sandwich spread. At the restaurant we serve it warm open-faced on baguettes with tomato and cucumber slices on top.

Gnocchi Parmesan

Made with cream puff dough, these gnocchi are lighter and fluffier than the traditional Italian potato dumplings. Serve this comforting dish before a simple grilled entrée or as a main course with a watercress salad and a glass of red wine.

6 appetizers or 4 entrées

1 cup milk

7 tablespoons unsalted butter

¾ teaspoon salt

¾ cup all-purpose flour

4 eggs

2 cups heavy cream

1 cup (4 ounces) freshly grated Parmesan cheese

¼ teaspoon freshly ground black pepper

chopped fresh chives for garnish

Because you will need to cook the gnocchi quickly once the batter is ready, do the following before you begin the preparation. Bring a large stockpot of salted water to a boil and reduce to a simmer. Have a large bowl of iced water nearby.

Combine milk, butter, and ½ teaspoon salt in a medium-heavy saucepan. Bring to boil over high heat. Add flour and stir vigorously with a wooden spoon until mixture is nearly solid, about 2 minutes. The batter should be the consistency of mashed potatoes and should clear the sides of the pan to form a ball. Remove from heat.

Transfer to a large bowl and add eggs, one at a time, beating well after each addition. (An electric mixer is fine for this.) The batter should be very thick, shiny, and smooth. Fill a pastry bag, fitted with a large plain tip #8, with batter.

Holding pastry bag over simmering water, gently squeeze out dough, slicing into 1-inch lengths with a paring knife.

Working in 4 batches of about 20 pieces, cook gnocchi at a slow simmer, stirring occasionally, until they start to puff, about 5 minutes. They should resemble floating corks. To test for doneness, remove a dumpling and cut in half. The center should have tiny bubbles. With a slotted spoon, transfer gnocchi to the bowl of iced water to cool.

Drain well in a colander. At this stage, you can store gnocchi in refrigerator up to 2 days.

Preheat oven to 450°F.

Bring cream to a boil in a medium ovenproof skillet or casserole. Add Parmesan, pepper, ¼ teaspoon salt, and gnocchi. Return to a boil and transfer to oven. Bake until sauce is thick and bubbly and a slight crust forms on top, about 7 minutes. Garnish with chopped chives and serve immediately.

Fried Brie with Tomato Coulis

This dish is a sensual combination of mild, runny cheese, crisp breading, and sweet, smooth tomato sauce. The key lies in working with ice-cold cheese, so it keeps its shape when it hits the hot oil.

6 servings

1½ pounds Brie cheese
3 eggs
1 cup all-purpose flour
1 cup fine dry bread crumbs
4 cups peanut oil for frying
Tomato Coulis, recipe follows

Slice Brie into 6 wedges and refrigerate until very cold and firm. Beat eggs in a bowl and place flour and bread crumbs in individual bowls. When cheese is cold, dip each wedge, one at a time, in flour, patting off any excess. Then dip in eggs, drain, and coat with bread crumbs. Be meticulous about covering every spot of cheese. Reserve coated cheese on a platter in freezer for 10 minutes.

Dip each wedge in eggs and bread crumbs again, being careful to drain the eggs and thoroughly coat with bread crumbs. Place in freezer for another 10 minutes.

Preheat oven to 350°F.

Heat oil in a large stockpot or saucepan to deep-fry temperature (350°F). Fry wedges, three at a time, until golden brown, about 1 minute. Do not stir, since the breading is easily broken. Carefully remove with a slotted spoon and drain on paper towels. Transfer to a large roasting pan and bake for 5 minutes.

To serve, coat each plate with warm Tomato Coulis. Top with wedge of cheese and serve immediately.

Variation: For cocktail parties, follow the same procedure with cheese cut into ½-inch cubes.

Tomato Coulis

This smooth tomato puree made with Madeira is sweet and mellow.

makes 2 cups

3 tablespoons unsalted butter
½ small onion, thinly sliced
3 mushrooms, thinly sliced
2 shallots, thinly sliced
1 small leek, white part, thinly sliced
¼ teaspoon salt
1 tablespoon brandy
¼ cup plus 1 tablespoon Madeira
1 cup chicken stock or canned broth
3 ripe tomatoes, chopped with skins
2 sprigs thyme
1 bay leaf
salt and freshly ground black pepper to taste

Melt 2 tablespoons butter in a medium skillet over low heat. Cook onion, mushrooms, shallots, leek, and salt until soft, about 7 minutes. Add brandy and ¼ cup Madeira. Turn heat to high and light alcohol with a match. Cook over high heat until liquid is reduced by half.

Add chicken stock, tomatoes, thyme, and bay leaf. Reduce the heat to low and simmer, uncovered, for 20 minutes. Puree in a food processor or blender and strain.

Return to pan and place over medium heat. Whisk in remaining tablespoon butter, broken in small pieces, and remaining tablespoon Madeira. Season with salt and pepper to taste and serve.

Zucchini Pancakes with Tomato Concassé

This vegetable pancake becomes light and fluffy as the eggs gently cook. It's a favorite among vegetarians and makes a lovely brunch dish served with a green salad and good, fresh bread.

6 appetizers or 2 entreés

1 large zucchini, ends trimmed and roughly grated with skins
3 eggs
3 tablespoons chopped parsley leaves
¾ teaspoon salt
½ teaspoon freshly ground black pepper
2 tablespoons unsalted butter
Tomato Concassé, recipe follows
freshly grated Parmesan cheese for garnish

Preheat broiler.

Mix zucchini, eggs, parsley, salt, and pepper in a medium bowl. Melt 1 tablespoon butter in each of 2 small ovenproof skillets (preferably Teflon) over medium-high heat. Pour half the zucchini mixture into each skillet and reduce heat to low. Gently cook, shaking pan occasionally, until batter is loose in center and set around the edges, 3 to 5 minutes.

Transfer to broiler and cook until firm in center, but not browned, about 4 minutes.

To serve, slice each into 3 wedges and center on serving plates. Garnish with warm Tomato Concassé and Parmesan cheese, and serve immediately.

Tomato Concassé

This peasant sauce—
roughly chopped and
quickly cooked—makes
a lively garnish for
grilled vegetables.

3 tablespoons olive oil

1 medium onion, diced

2 garlic cloves, minced

1 teaspoon salt

3 ripe large tomatoes, peeled, seeded, and diced (page 236) or
    6 canned Italian plum tomatoes, seeds removed

5 bay leaves

1 teaspoon chopped fresh thyme or ½ teaspoon dried

1 teaspoon freshly ground black pepper

Heat oil in a medium skillet over moderate heat. Sauté onions, garlic, and salt until golden, about 10 minutes. Add tomatoes, bay leaves, thyme, and pepper. Reduce to a simmer and cook, uncovered, stirring occasionally, 15 to 20 minutes. Remove and discard bay leaves, and serve. Concassé may be stored in refrigerator up to a week.

makes 2 cups

Avocado Grapefruit Salad with Sour Cream–Honey Dressing

The grapefruit and avocado slices for this easy salad can be arranged in advance and refrigerated. To avoid breaking down the fruit, add the dressing right before serving. Leftover dressing is excellent on summer fruit salads.

6 servings

3 pink grapefruits, chilled
3 ripe medium avocados, halved, seeded, and peeled
¾ cup sour cream
juice of 2 large limes
3 tablespoons honey
½ teaspoon salt
¼ teaspoon freshly ground black pepper
mint leaves for garnish

Slice ends off grapefruits and stand upright on a counter. Cut away skin and membrane, exposing fruit. Working over a bowl to catch the juice, separate sections by slicing with a serrated knife between membranes. Remove and discard seeds. Slice avocado halves lengthwise in ½-inch slices. Arrange alternating grapefruit sections and avocado slices on 6 salad plates.

Whisk together sour cream, lime juice, honey, salt, and pepper in a small bowl. Just before serving, spoon about 2 tablespoons dressing in a stripe over each salad. Garnish with mint leaves and serve.

Variation: Toss chunks of avocado and supremes of grapefruit with salt, pepper, and olive oil.

2 Soups and Stocks

We aren't sure why people don't cook more soups at home. We suspect it has something to do with the mistaken notion that a soup has to simmer for a long time in order to taste good. Actually, some of our favorite creamed soups can be prepared in about half an hour. In fact, the key to their intense tastes lies in cooking the main ingredient very briefly, so the pure flavor shines through. Ultimately, homemade soups *are* convenient. They can be cooked in advance and reheated whenever you need a nourishing lunch or hearty starter.

One precaution: Keep in mind that the quantities of salt in the recipes are based on using homemade chicken stock. Adjust the amount accordingly if substituting a salty canned broth.

Creamed Soups

Creamed vegetable soups offer the stomach-filling satisfaction we sometimes yearn for in a soup. With their rich flavors and velvety consistency they can serve admirably as either starters or entrées, depending on the serving size. Don't hesitate to reduce the amount of cream in the recipes to suit your taste or diet. Half and half or milk may be substituted as desired.

Cream of Mushroom Soup

4 tablespoons (½ stick) unsalted butter
1½ pounds mushrooms, cleaned and thinly sliced
1 tablespoon salt
1 teaspoon freshly ground black pepper
3 cups chicken stock or canned broth
2 cups heavy cream
1 tablespoon plus 1 teaspoon fresh lemon juice

Melt butter over high heat in a large stockpot or Dutch oven. Cook mushrooms, uncovered, with salt and pepper until nearly all moisture is evaporated, about 15 minutes.

Stir in chicken stock and cream, bring to a boil, and remove from heat. Puree in a blender until smooth. Return to pot and bring just to a boil. Remove from heat. Add lemon juice, season with salt and pepper to taste, and serve immediately.

There is little to distract from the clean, pure taste of mushrooms in this rich soup. Since they are so absorbent, the best way to clean mushrooms is by wiping with a damp cloth or paper towel rather than immersing in water. You can slice the mushrooms roughly by hand or with the slicing disk in a food processor. Precision isn't important since they will be pureed later.

6 to 8 servings

Tomato and Fennel Soup

This is the most elegant and refined of our creamed vegetable soups. It's sweet and delicate, allowing a hearty entrée like Marinated Rib Eye with Gorgonzola Sauce (page 76) to follow.

6 to 8 servings

1 large fennel bulb with stems and leaves
2 tablespoons unsalted butter
1 medium onion, thinly sliced
2 teaspoons salt
½ teaspoon freshly ground black pepper
½ cup Pernod
2 to 3 ripe tomatoes, seeded, and chopped (page 236)
2 cups chicken stock or canned broth
½ cup heavy cream
½ cup half and half
dash of Tabasco

Wash and trim fennel, discarding stems. Separate bulb into stalks and thinly slice. Reserve wispy inner leaves for garnish.

Melt butter over moderate heat in a large stockpot or Dutch oven. Cook onions with salt and pepper until soft, about 10 minutes. Add fennel, reduce heat to low, and cook an additional 5 minutes.

Turn heat to high and add Pernod. (Don't be alarmed if the alcohol flames. It will subside momentarily.) Cook until liquid is reduced by half. Add tomatoes and chicken stock. Reduce to a simmer and cook, covered, about 15 minutes.

Puree in a blender until smooth. Strain back into pot and add cream and half and half. Bring to a boil, remove from heat, and stir in Tabasco. Serve immediately, garnished with fresh fennel leaves.

Butternut Squash Soup

This basic creamed squash soup makes a terrific autumn lunch served with plenty of warm fresh bread and a green salad.

6 servings

1 large butternut squash, about 1½ pounds, cut in half lengthwise and seeded
2 tablespoons unsalted butter
2 medium onions, sliced
1½ teaspoons salt
¾ teaspoon freshly ground black pepper
4 cups chicken stock or canned broth
1 cup heavy cream
1 cup half and half
1 lime for garnish

Preheat oven to 450°F. Bake squash, cut-side down, in a foil covered roasting pan with about 1-inch water, until soft, 45 to 60 minutes. When cool enough to handle, scrape out interior flesh and reserve.

Melt butter over moderate heat in a large stockpot or Dutch oven. Sauté onions with salt and pepper until golden, 10 to 15 minutes. Add squash and chicken stock. Bring to a boil, reduce to a simmer, and cook, uncovered, about 10 minutes.

Puree in a blender until smooth. Strain back into pot and add cream and half and half. Return to a boil and remove from heat.

Peel lime and remove sections. (Follow the method used for lemons, page 199.)Dice into small pieces. Serve soup immediately, garnished with diced lime.

Yam and Ginger Soup

This soup reminds us of sweet potato pie without the crust. It is so sweet and thick. It would make a great opener for a winter dinner of Turkey Breast with Lemon Butter (page 100) and Sautéed Mustard Greens (page 169).

4 to 6 servings

1 to 2 large yams, about 2 pounds
2 tablespoons unsalted butter
1½ medium onions, sliced
2½ teaspoons salt
½ teaspoon freshly ground black pepper
3 tablespoons freshly grated ginger (page 236)
3 cups chicken stock or canned broth
1 cup heavy cream
1 cup half and half
juice of ½ lime

Preheat oven to 350°F. Bake yam until thoroughly soft, about 1 hour. (The sugar will rise to the surface and form syrup droplets on the yam's skin when done.) When cool enough to handle, peel and cut into slices.

Melt butter over medium-low heat in a large stockpot or Dutch oven. Cook onions with salt and pepper until soft, about 10 minutes. Add ginger and cook an additional 3 minutes, stirring occasionally. Add yams and chicken stock. Bring to a boil, reduce to a simmer, and cook, uncovered, 10 minutes.

Puree in a blender until smooth. Strain back into pot and stir in cream and half and half. Bring to a boil and remove from heat. Stir in lime juice and serve immediately.

Cream of Lettuce Soup

This is the best use we know for leftover or wilted salad greens. Virtually any lettuce will do, including spinach or watercress, but try to anticipate the final result, since a bitter green may yield a soup that is too tart for your taste.

4 to 6 servings

2 tablespoons unsalted butter

1½ medium onions, sliced

1 slice bacon

1½ teaspoons salt

½ teaspoon freshly ground black pepper

1 medium red potato, peeled and thinly sliced

4 cups chicken stock or canned broth

1 large or 2 small heads lettuce, leaves separated, washed, and
   roughly chopped into small pieces

1 cup heavy cream

1 cup half and half

Melt butter over medium-low heat in a large stockpot or Dutch oven. Cook onions with bacon, salt, and pepper until soft, about 10 minutes. Add potato and chicken stock. Bring to a boil, reduce to a simmer and cook, uncovered, about 15 minutes.

Remove and discard bacon. Return stock to a boil, reduce to a simmer, and stir in lettuce. Cook over moderate heat, uncovered, 3 to 4 minutes.

Puree in blender until smooth. Strain back into pot, pressing with a ladle to extract all juices. Stir in cream and half and half. Bring to a boil and remove from heat. Serve immediately.

Variation: For a thinner lettuce soup, use romaine and omit the cream and half and half. Garnish with a mixture of ¼ cup each Gorgonzola cheese and sour cream and 1 teaspoon cracked pepper.

Hearty Broths

These rustic peasant soups are dearest to our hearts. While each has its own special charm, all are substantial and interesting enough to serve alone as a lunch or light dinner with nothing more than a salad, some bread, and wine.

Black-Eyed Pea Soup

Black-eyed peas, or cowpeas, are less starchy and more flavorful than other dried beans. In all our bean soups we call for boiling rather than soaking the beans to soften them. These techniques can be used interchangeably.

8 servings

2 cups dry black-eyed peas, washed
4 slices bacon, cut in small squares
2 medium onions, diced
2 stalks of celery, diced
1 teaspoon salt
½ teaspoon freshly ground black pepper
6 cups chicken stock or canned broth
1 sprig fresh rosemary
1 tomato, peeled, seeded, and diced (page 236)

Place beans in a medium saucepan and cover with a generous quantity of water. Bring to a boil and cook, uncovered, until beans are tender, about 1 hour. Drain and reserve.

Cook bacon in a large stockpot over low heat until tender, not crisp. Add onions, celery, salt, and pepper. Cook over low heat until vegetables are soft, about 10 minutes.

Add peas, chicken stock, and rosemary. Bring to a boil, reduce to a simmer, and cook, uncovered, 30 minutes. Remove and discard the rosemary, stir in tomatoes, and cook long enough to heat through. Serve immediately.

Swiss Onion Soup

Unlike some onion soups where the cheese forms a tough, stringy mass at the top, the cheese in this hearty soup grows softer and sweeter as it simmers in the milky broth. It may not look great, but the taste is superb. You can refrigerate this homey soup for as long as 6 days with no loss of quality. When gently reheating it, remember to keep stirring.

8 to 10 servings

8 tablespoons (1 stick) unsalted butter
3 medium onions, thinly sliced
2 teaspoons salt
¼ teaspoon freshly ground black pepper
½ loaf day-old French bread or 6 slices white bread
1 teaspoon granulated sugar
2 quarts milk
1 pound good-quality Swiss or Gruyère cheese, diced

Melt butter over moderate heat in a large heavy stockpot or Dutch oven. Cook onions with salt and pepper until soft but not colored, 15 minutes.

Cut bread into medium dice and add to pot along with sugar. Stir constantly for about 1 minute, so bread absorbs butter.

Add milk and bring to a boil. Add cheese, stir, and reduce to a simmer. Cook, uncovered, stirring occasionally, about 1 hour 15 minutes. Serve immediately.

Lentil Soup

In this authentic Indian recipe, the onions and lentils are well browned before the stock is added. The resulting broth is thick and earthy, with a lovely caramel color. You can easily adapt this recipe for vegetarians by substituting water for the chicken stock.

6 servings

2 tablespoons unsalted butter

1 large onion, diced

1 teaspoon salt

2 tablespoons pureed garlic (page 236)

1½ tablespoons freshly grated ginger (page 235)

¼ teaspoon freshly ground black pepper

1½ cups lentils, washed and drained

5 cups chicken stock, canned broth, or water

plain yogurt for garnish

Melt butter over medium-high heat in a large stockpot or Dutch oven. Sauté onions with salt until deep brown, about 10 minutes. Reduce heat to low and add garlic, ginger, and pepper. Cook until aromas are released, stirring constantly, about 2 minutes. Add lentils and cook an additional 3 minutes, constantly stirring so the beans are evenly cooked.

Add chicken stock, bring to a boil, reduce to a simmer, and cook, uncovered, about 1 hour 15 minutes. Stir soup regularly to ensure even cooking so that beans do not burn. When done, beans should be soft inside, with no chalkiness. Serve immediately, garnished with a dollop of yogurt.

Thai Pork Dumpling Soup

This is the kind of one-dish meal we love to eat. The broth is clear and strong with the distinctive tastes of black pepper and cilantro, and the bowl is brimming with interesting textures. Don't be daunted by the unusual ingredients—this is a simple dish to prepare.

10 servings

THAI PESTO

½ bunch fresh cilantro, stems removed

½ tablespoon palm sugar (page 234) or brown sugar

½ tablespoon freshly grated ginger (page 235)

1 teaspoon cracked black pepper

1 teaspoon pureed garlic (page 236)

1 tablespoon Thai Fish Sauce (page 235)

1 ounce cellophane noodles or bean threads (page 233)

¼ pound fresh or dried black fungus (wood ear mushrooms)
   (page 232)

10 ounces ground pork

1 tablespoon Thai Fish Sauce (page 235)

1 teaspoon pureed garlic (page 236)

1 tablespoon cornstarch

10 cups chicken stock or canned broth

freshly ground black pepper and Thai Fish Sauce to taste

1 bunch scallions, white and green parts, thinly sliced

½ bunch cilantro, leaves only

To make pesto, puree all ingredients in a food processor or blender until a fine paste is formed. Set aside. You can do this by hand by first chopping all ingredients, except Thai Fish Sauce, together on a board to form a paste. Then mix with fish sauce in a small bowl.

Follow directions on packages for reconstituting cellophane noodles and dried mushrooms, if necessary. Noodles usually need to soak in warm water for about 15 minutes; mushrooms about 30 minutes.

While ingredients are soaking, make dumplings by combining ground pork, Thai Fish Sauce, garlic, and cornstarch in a bowl. With your hands, form small meatballs, about the size of hazelnuts. Set aside.

When noodles and mushrooms are finished soaking, drain. Remove and discard the tough stems and slice mushrooms into julienne strips. Cut noodles into 2- to 3-inch lengths.

Place all ingredients near stove and bring chicken stock to a boil in a large stockpot. Reduce to a simmer and add pork balls, mushrooms, and noodles. Cook, uncovered, until pork is done, about 10 minutes. Stir in pesto and adjust seasonings with pepper and Thai Fish Sauce. (We like this broth really peppery.) Ladle into serving bowls, sprinkle with sliced scallions and cilantro leaves, and serve immediately.

Pistou

All the flavors of the garden ring out loud and clear in this light vegetable soup from southern France. You can substitute any vegetables that are available, or omit some, but make sure to have fresh basil on hand for the dollop of Pesto. We like to serve this fragrant broth topped with poached and sliced chicken breast at lunchtime.

The key to a good vegetable soup is twofold. First, chop the vegetables evenly, then add them to the pot in the proper sequence. Harder vegetables (like potatoes and carrots) always precede softer vegetables (like tomatoes and zucchini), so they all cook to the same degree of tenderness.

6 servings

⅓ cup dry white beans (navy or great northern), washed

PESTO

2 garlic cloves, peeled

3 tablespoons extra virgin olive oil

1 bunch fresh basil, leaves only

1 cup (4 ounces) freshly grated Gruyère or Parmesan cheese

2 small red potatoes, with skins

1 large carrot, peeled

1 small onion

1 small zucchini, with skin

1 small yellow crookneck squash, with skin

1 stalk of celery, peeled

1 large tomato, peeled, and seeded (page 236)

¼ pound green beans

8 cups chicken stock or canned broth

salt and freshly ground black pepper to taste

Place beans in a small saucepan and cover with a generous amount of water. Bring to a boil and cook, uncovered, until beans are tender, about 1 hour. Drain and reserve. (To test a bean for doneness, choose a small one. Smaller beans take longer to cook because of their dense centers. The bean should taste creamy, rather than powdery, inside.)

Make Pesto by pureeing garlic, olive oil, and a few basil leaves in a blender. Gradually add remaining leaves until all are pureed. Transfer to a small bowl, add grated cheese, and stir. Set aside.

Cut each vegetable into even ½-inch dice and set aside. To avoid discoloration, reserve potatoes in a bowl of cold water.

Bring chicken stock to a boil in a large stockpot. Add white beans, potatoes, carrot, and onion. Return to a boil, reduce to a simmer, and cook, uncovered, 15 minutes. Add remaining vegetables and bring back to boil. Reduce to a simmer and cook an additional 10 minutes, uncovered. Season to taste with salt and pepper.

To serve, place a generous tablespoon Pesto in each bowl, add soup, and serve immediately.

Cold Soups

Cold soups are wonderful for warm-weather entertaining. They can be prepared well in advance, then set in the refrigerator to chill while you prepare the rest of the meal or just relax. They're the ideal starter for summer barbecues as well as elegant dinner parties. And, they pack well for picnics.

Cucumber Yogurt Soup

This quick summer soup has just enough cumin and garlic to keep it from being ordinary. Be fussy about choosing cucumbers, since their flavor will determine the overall quality of this dish. We prefer the smaller, pale green pickling cukes called Kirbies to larger salad cucumbers. Always trim and discard the ends of cucumbers, where the bitter oils collect.

6 servings

6 large pickling cucumbers or Kirbies (page 234), peeled and roughly chopped
2 teaspoons salt
½ teaspoon freshly ground black pepper
1½ teaspoons pureed garlic (page 236)
1½ teaspoons ground cumin
3 cups plain yogurt
chopped fresh mint leaves for garnish

Puree cucumbers, salt, pepper, garlic, cumin, and yogurt in a blender until smooth. Strain through a medium sieve and chill a minimum of 2 hours. Serve cold, garnished with mint.

Cold Sorrel Soup

Cooking the sorrel quickly, then combining it with minimal amount of stock preserves its elusive lemony flavor beautifully. This is an excellent choice for a summer dinner party where you plan to serve a strong-tasting meat like duck or lamb. This soup can also be served hot.

6 servings

2 tablespoons unsalted butter
1 large onion, thinly sliced
2 teaspoons salt
¼ teaspoon freshly ground black pepper
6 bunches sorrel, stems trimmed and washed
1½ cups half and half
2 cups water
dash of Tabasco
1 teaspoon fresh lemon juice

Melt butter over moderate heat in a medium stockpot or Dutch oven. Cook onion with salt and pepper until soft, about 15 minutes. Stir in sorrel and cook over moderate heat, uncovered, about 5 minutes. Stir occasionally so the sorrel is evenly cooked.

Add half and half, water, and Tabasco. Bring to a boil and remove from heat. Puree in a blender until smooth and strain through a medium sieve. Stir in lemon juice, adjust with salt and pepper, and refrigerate a minimum of 4 hours, or, to serve immediately, chill in bowl rested in another bowl of iced water. Serve cold.

Gazpacho

Our favorite cold soup—this smooth Gazpacho—is dressier and takes less time to prepare than the chunkier version. The vegetables can be randomly chopped since they are pureed in the food processor before being combined with a rich mayonnaise.

6 to 8 servings

1 stalk of celery, chopped

1 tomato, cored and quartered

1 small green bell pepper, cored and seeded

1 large cucumber or 4 pickling cucumbers or Kirbies (page 234), peeled and chopped

5 garlic cloves, peeled

1 to 2 small jalapeño peppers, seeds optional to taste

2 slices day-old white bread, crusts removed

1 (32-ounce) can tomato juice

MAYONNAISE

3 egg yolks

1 tablespoon paprika

2 tablespoons tarragon vinegar or white wine vinegar

1½ teaspoons salt

1 cup olive oil

Tabasco to taste

chopped fresh chives for garnish

Process celery, tomato, bell pepper, cucumber, garlic, jalapeños, and bread in a food processor until fine. Transfer to a blender along with tomato juice and puree in batches until smooth. Strain and set aside.

Make Mayonnaise by whisking together egg yolks, paprika, vinegar, and salt in a large bowl. Gradually add olive oil, one drop at a time, whisking constantly until an emulsion forms. (As the mixture thickens, you can begin adding the oil faster.) After Mayonnaise is formed, start adding reserved vegetable puree ¼ cup at a time, *whisking constantly*, until thoroughly blended. Adjust with Tabasco and chill for a minimum of 2 hours. Serve in chilled bowls, with a sprinkling of chopped chives.

Cold Avocado Soup with Fresh Tomato Salsa

This refreshing summer soup is as smooth and lovely as a ripe avocado. It is best served the same day, since avocados discolor quickly. For vegetarians, substitute water for the chicken stock.

6 to 8 servings

3 ripe avocados, halved, peeled, and seeded
2 tablespoons olive oil
1 medium onion, thinly sliced
2 cups chicken stock, canned broth, or water
2 cups milk
1½ teaspoons salt
dash of freshly ground black pepper
2 tablespoons fresh lime juice
Fresh Tomato Salsa for garnish, recipe follows

Roughly chop avocados and place in a large bowl.

Heat oil over low heat in a large saucepan. Cook onions until soft, about 10 minutes. Add chicken stock, turn the heat to high, and bring to a boil. Then, pour over avocados and mix to combine.

Transfer to a blender and puree with remaining ingredients until smooth. Strain and chill for a minimum of 2 hours. Serve cold, garnished with a heaping tablespoon Fresh Tomato Salsa.

Fresh Tomato Salsa

2 tomatoes with skins, seeds removed, and finely diced
1 small red onion, finely diced
1 to 3 serrano chiles, with seeds, finely diced
1 bunch fresh cilantro, stems trimmed and chopped
1 teaspoon salt
2 tablespoons fresh lime juice

makes 1 cup

Mix ingredients together in a bowl and chill.

Seafood Soups

From the elegant Crayfish or Lobster Bisque (page 50) to the stout Geoduck Clam Chowder (page 49), each of these shellfish soups is a gem. They are a bit more demanding to prepare than other soups. Save them for an occasion when expectations are high and time is plentiful. ✕

Clams in Cream and Thyme Broth

This is one of the simplest and best ways to cook clams. Just throw the ingredients into a pot and within minutes the shells are open and the cream is infused with the taste of the ocean and the earthy aroma of thyme. Use small tender clams, such as cockles or Manilla, for this dish. Littlenecks will do, but they are not quite as tender.

4 to 6 servings

60 clams, in the shell
1 cup clam juice or fish stock (page 56)
2 cups heavy cream
2 bunches fresh thyme, leaves only, roughly chopped
½ teaspoon freshly ground black pepper
salt to taste

Wash clams in cold running water and scrub with a brush to remove surface sand.

Place clams in a large saucepan with clam juice, cream, thyme, and pepper. Cover and cook over high heat, shaking occasionally, until shells open, 4 to 6 minutes. Remove from heat. Season with salt to taste. Ladle into soup bowls and serve at once.

Crayfish or Lobster Bisque

We learned this wonderfully refined bisque while working at Le Perroquet in Chicago, where we each cooked the restaurant's signature dish hundreds of times. We can't imagine ever growing tired of its silken texture and complex flavor. It's pure heaven in a bowl.

6 to 8 servings

2 tablespoons unsalted butter
12 shallots, thinly sliced
12 mushrooms, thinly sliced
1 cup brandy
1 cup Madeira
6 cups Lobster or Crayfish Stock (page 52)

BEURRE MANIÉ

1 tablespoon softened, unsalted butter
2 tablespoons all-purpose flour

1½ cups heavy cream
¼ teaspoon fresh lemon juice
dash of Tabasco

Melt butter in a large stockpot over medium-high heat. Sauté shallots until golden, about 3 minutes. Add mushrooms and cook over high heat until slightly browned, about 2 additional minutes.

Remove from heat and add brandy and Madeira, reserving ¼ cup of each for final seasoning. Cook over high heat until liquid is reduced by half. Add Lobster or Crayfish Stock and return to a boil. Reduce to a simmer and cook, uncovered, 15 to 30 minutes, depending on the strength of your stock. (Weaker stocks need to cook longer to concentrate their flavors.) Occasionally skim and discard foam that rises to top.

Make *beurre manié* by mixing butter and flour together with your fingers to form a smooth paste. Press onto ends of a whisk.

When broth has a strong, almost salty, lobster or crayfish flavor, add cream and bring it back to a boil, skimming foam occasionally. Then whisk in *beurre manié* until dissolved. Cook an additional 5 minutes over high heat, whisking occasionally.

Geoduck Clam Chowder

*This sturdy broth is
filled with the pure taste
of clams. Geoducks,
which measure about
one foot from side to
side and are available
at specialty fish markets
in most Chinatowns,
have the most
remarkable flavor we
have ever tasted.*

6 servings

10 ounces fresh clam meat, preferably geoduck, cut in 1-inch pieces
4 tablespoons (½ stick) unsalted butter
1½ medium onions, diced
4 cups clam juice
2 cups heavy cream
1 large carrot, peeled and diced
1 stalk of celery, diced
1 large red or white potato, peeled and diced

BEURRE MANIÉ
½ tablespoon softened, unsalted butter
1 tablespoon all-purpose flour

½ teaspoon salt
¼ teaspoon freshly ground black pepper
2 dashes of Tabasco
juice of ½ lemon

Grind clam meat in a meat grinder through large holes or food processor until roughly chopped and reserve.

Melt butter in a large stockpot over low heat. Cook onions until soft, about 5 minutes. Add clams and cook an additional 3 minutes, stirring occasionally to avoid browning.

Add clam juice, turn heat to high, and bring to a boil. Add cream, return to a boil, then reduce to a simmer. Add carrots, celery, and potato. Cook over medium-low heat, uncovered, until vegetables are tender, about 10 minutes.

Make *beurre manié* by mixing butter and flour together with your fingers to form a smooth paste. Press onto ends of a whisk and stir into soup until completely and evenly dispersed. Stir in remaining ingredients, taste and adjust seasonings, and serve immediately.

Strain through a fine sieve, pressing with the back of a ladle to extract all juices. Season with lemon juice, reserved brandy and Madeira, and Tabasco, and serve immediately.

Lobster and Vegetable Broth

There is nothing precious about this rich lobster broth. It is densely packed with noodles, vegetables, and large chunks of lobster or crayfish. What a great surprise to serve at a special lunch or light dinner with loaves of crusty French bread and a salad.

8 appetizers or 4 entrées

3 ounces vermicelli
6¾ cups Lobster or Crayfish Stock (page 52)
3 ounces Chinese snow peas or green beans, trimmed and julienned lengthwise
1 leek, white part, washed, cut in half, and thinly sliced across the width
1 large carrot, peeled and finely julienned
reserved lobster or crayfish meat from stock making (page 52)
4 tablespoons (½ stick) unsalted butter, cold
3 tablespoons balsamic or sherry wine vinegar

Bring a medium saucepan of salted water to a boil. Cook vermicelli just until al dente. Drain in colander and rinse with cold water. Reserve.

Combine Lobster or Crayfish Stock with vegetables in a large stockpot and bring to a boil. While stock is heating, cut reserved lobster tail into ½-inch slices, leaving claws whole. Add lobster or crayfish to stock and return to a boil.

Dip vermicelli into broth to warm. Divide vermicelli among serving bowls. Remove lobster meat with a slotted spoon and place on vermicelli. Ladle over broth, and garnish each with pea-sized pieces cold butter and an equal share of balsamic vinegar. Serve immediately.

Lobster or Crayfish Stock

This basic shellfish stock forms the base for Lobster and Vegetable Broth (page 51) and Crayfish or Lobster Bisque (page 50), as well as classic lobster sauce. We use lobster and crayfish interchangeably, although lobster has a slightly richer flavor. The stock can be refrigerated for up to 2 days or frozen indefinitely. Oftentimes, you'll find yourself with only a few lobster bodies. In that case, wrap well and reserve in the freezer until you've gathered 10 to 12.

makes 6¾ cups

4 (1½-pound) lobsters or 4 pounds crayfish
8 tablespoons (1 stick) unsalted butter
¼ cup olive oil
2 medium onions, finely chopped
2 carrots, peeled and chopped
2 stalks celery, peeled and chopped
1½ teaspoons salt
2 cups dry white wine
1 cup Madeira
5 cups Fish Stock (page 56), clam juice, or water
3 cups tomato juice
1 head garlic, with skins, cut in half horizontally
½ bunch fresh parsley, with stems
1 tablespoon black peppercorns
2 bay leaves
1½ teaspoons dried tarragon
1 teaspoon dried thyme
½ teaspoon cayenne pepper

Bring a large stockpot of water to a rolling boil, add lobsters, and cook at a fast boil until done, about 10 minutes. Transfer to a bowl of iced water to cool, then remove and reserve tail and claw meat for another use. Do this messy job over a bowl to reserve drippings. Crush shells, which will be the base for the stock, using a mallet or hammer, then grind as fine as possible with reserved drippings in a food processor.

Follow same procedure for crayfish, reserving tail meat and claws, if possible, then grinding shells.

Melt butter and oil in a large stockpot over medium-high heat. Cook onions, carrots, celery, and salt until golden, about 10 minutes.

Stir in crushed shells, white wine, and Madeira. Turn heat to high and cook until liquid is reduced by half.

Add Fish Stock and tomato juice. Bring to a boil and carefully skim and discard foam that rises to surface. Add remaining ingredients and cook at a simmer, uncovered, 1 hour 15 minutes.

Strain through a fine sieve and refrigerate up to 2 days or freeze indefinitely.

Mussel Bisque

If you haven't cooked a bisque before, this one is good to begin with. Mussels are easy to work with, and this recipe doesn't call for a homemade stock. Try to dice the vegetables as finely as possible, so they don't distract from the sweet silkiness of this fine bisque.

6 servings

2 cups dry white wine
1½ pounds mussels, washed and debearded (page 235)
1 tablespoon unsalted butter
4 mushrooms, thinly sliced
4 shallots, thinly sliced
½ teaspoon salt
½ teaspoon freshly ground black pepper
½ cup plus 1 tablespoon applejack or apple brandy
3 cups clam juice
3 cups heavy cream

BEURRE MANIÉ
½ tablespoon softened, unsalted butter
1 tablespoon all-purpose flour

1 small red potato, with skin, finely diced
1 small stalk of celery, finely diced
½ carrot, peeled and finely diced
1 teaspoon fresh lemon juice
dash of Tabasco

(*continued*)

Bring wine to a boil in a large saucepan. Add mussels, reduce to a simmer, and cook, covered, until shells open, about 4 minutes. Remove mussels and set aside to cool, covered with a wet towel. Strain remaining liquid through a layer of cheesecloth or towel, to remove sand, and reserve.

Melt butter in a large stockpot or Dutch oven over low heat. Cook mushrooms and shallots with salt and pepper until soft, about 5 minutes. Add ½ cup applejack, turn heat to high, and cook until liquid is reduced by half. Add clam juice and reserved liquid, and reduce by a quarter. Add cream and bring to a boil.

Meanwhile make *beurre manié* by mixing butter and flour together with your fingers to form a smooth paste. Press onto ends of a whisk.

When liquid is boiling, quickly whisk in *beurre manié* until completely and evenly dispersed. Simmer an additional 5 minutes, remove from heat, and strain. Return to pot, add remaining diced vegetables, and bring back to a boil, simmer until potatoes are tender, then remove from heat. Season with lemon juice, Tabasco, remaining tablespoon of applejack, and salt and pepper to taste.

Remove mussels from their shells and stir into the warm soup. Ladle into serving bowls and garnish each with an open shell.

Stocks

A full-bodied stock is indispensable for making terrific soups and sauces. At the restaurant, we begin each day by starting a 20-gallon pot of chicken stock and end by putting up 15-gallon pots of the brown stocks, to bubble through the night. Stocks should be as fresh and flavorful as every other ingredient.

For the best results, start with fresh vegetables. Always cook at a gentle simmer, not a boil, and skim the foam, or impurities, that rise to the top. Cook the approximate time called for, since it *is* possible to overcook stock, thereby muddling its flavors.

Before you eliminate the salt in these recipes, remember the amount in the finished product is minimal since the quantity is dispersed throughout about a gallon of stock. This salt extracts flavor from the aromatics and bones, and also acts as a preservative for stocks that are stored.

What home cooks need to learn is just how valuable the shells and bones of the meats/fish we eat are. Each time you bone chicken, duck, etc., save the bones in the freezer and then make stock. All the flavor then locked in the bones, sinews, and tendons is what makes food taste *so* good.

Fish Stock

makes 2 quarts

2 tablespoons unsalted butter

1 medium white onion, sliced

1 celery stalk, sliced

1 leek, sliced, white and light green part only

8 shallots, sliced

½ bunch parsley

1 teaspoon salt

2 cups dry white wine

3 pounds fish bones, preferably non-oily type like halibut, bass, or snapper, washed and cut into chunks

5 bay leaves

1 teaspoon dried thyme

1 teaspoon dried tarragon

1 teaspoon cracked peppercorns (page 235)

Melt butter in a large heavy stockpot or saucepan over moderate heat. Cook onion, celery, leeks, shallots, parsley, and salt just until soft, about 5 minutes. Add wine, turn heat to high and reduce by half. Add bones and about 1½ gallons or enough water to cover. Bring to a boil. Skim off and discard foam that rises to top. Add remaining spices and cook at a simmer, uncovered, 1½ hours. Strain by lifting liquid out with a ladle. Discard solids. Set aside to cool to room temperature. Store in sealed containers in refrigerator 2 days or freeze indefinitely.

Strain by lifting liquid out with a ladle. Discard solids. Set aside to cool to room temperature and skim off any fat that rises to top. Brown stock may be kept in sealed containers in refrigerator up to a week or in freezer indefinitely.

Brown Duck Stock

Duck stock can be used in place of Brown Veal Stock in sauce making. It can also be a lovely base for a hearty barley or onion soup.

makes 3 quarts

carcasses, necks, feet, and heads from 2 ducks
2 carrots, peeled and cut into large chunks
2 medium onions, peeled and cut into quarters
2 celery stalks, roughly chopped
5 bay leaves
1 bunch fresh thyme or 2 teaspoons dried
½ bunch fresh tarragon or 1 teaspoon dried
1 bunch parsley stems
1 head garlic, cut in half horizontally
1 tablespoon black peppercorns
1 tablespoon salt

Preheat oven to 350°F. Crack bones with a heavy cleaver and arrange in one layer on large baking sheet or roasting pan. Bake ½ hour. Add carrots and onions, and bake for an additional 15 minutes. The bones and vegetables should turn a deep brown.

Combine roasted bones, carrots, onions, and celery in a large stockpot with enough water to cover, about 2 gallons. Bring to a vigorous boil. Skim and discard foam that rises to top. Reduce to a simmer, add spices and garlic, and cook, uncovered, skimming occasionally, for 3 hours.

Strain by lifting liquid out with a ladle. Discard solids. Set aside to cool to room temperature. Skim off any fat that rises to top. Duck stock may be kept in sealed containers in refrigerator up to 5 days or in freezer indefinitely. The layer of fat that rises to top may be saved and rendered (page 236) for sautéing.

Brown Lamb or Veal Stock

Like chicken, lamb bones make a delicious broth or base for stews and soups. Veal stock forms the foundation for a wide range of sauces for dark meats such as beef, veal, and liver.

makes 3 quarts

5 pounds lamb or veal bones (ask your butcher to crack the bones
    for stock making)
2 medium carrots, peeled and cut into large chunks
16 whole cloves
2 medium onions, with skins, cut in half horizontally
2 celery stalks, roughly chopped
1 head garlic, with skins, cut in half horizontally
1 leek, chopped
2 tomatoes, roughly chopped
2 cups dry white wine
1½ tablespoons salt
1 tablespoon dried thyme
1 tablespoon black peppercorns
1 teaspoon dried tarragon
6 bay leaves

Preheat oven to 400°F. Arrange bones in one layer in a roasting pan and roast for ½ hour, until some liquid has been released. (If the pan is dry, you can add about 2 tablespoons vegetable oil to speed up the process.) Then add carrots and bake an additional ½ hour, turning carrots occasionally, until bones and carrots are thoroughly browned.

Insert 4 cloves into each onion half. Heat a dry cast-iron skillet until very hot, then char onions, flat-side down, until black.

Combine roasted bones, carrots, onions, celery, garlic, leeks, and tomatoes in a large stockpot with white wine. Bring to boil and reduce to half. Add enough water to cover, about 2 gallons. Bring to a vigorous boil. Skim and discard foam that rises to the top. Reduce to a simmer, add remaining seasonings, and cook, uncovered, skimming occasionally. Lamb stock cooks about 4 hours and veal about 8.

(continued)

3 Sandwiches and Breads

While the "serious" restaurants where we received our training—like Ma Maison and Le Perroquet—traditionally ignore sandwiches, we decided to highlight them. We think many people would prefer a casual, quick meal to an appetizer and entrée in the middle of the day. We know we do.

Our sandwiches are big, messy affairs, bursting at the seams with contrasting tastes and textures. Most of them are made from ingredients we keep on hand and yet, each sandwich is special.

We hope our sandwiches will spark some ideas for using your favorite leftovers. Although sandwiches are considered a casual food, the details can make all the difference. Choose a flavorful bread and slice it thinly so people don't fill up on dough. Each bite must contain a taste of each ingredient. Serve sandwiches before they get soggy. Choose a few homemade condiments like sauerkraut, pickles, or a chutney to fill out the plate. Sandwich making (and eating) should be fun and we think these big, bold sandwiches illustrate that point well.

Sandwiches

Club Sandwich

Preheat grill. For 3 sandwiches, flatten 3 skinless, boneless slices of turkey breast (page 100). Salt and pepper generously and grill about 2 minutes per side. (Or, sauté the slices just as quickly in butter over high heat.) Cut a baguette into thirds crosswise, then in thirds lengthwise. Toast on grill or under broiler.

Fry 6 slices bacon until crisp.

Coat each slice bread with Horseradish and Mustard and Mayonnaise (page 178). On the 3 bottom pieces, place a serving of turkey, top with avocado slices, then the middle piece of bread. Cover each with 2 slices bacon, thinly sliced tomatoes, and green leaf lettuce. Top with remaining bread. Cut in half and serve with french fries, Cole Slaw (page 163), and pickles.

Fried Egg with Canadian Bacon and Mustard Greens

For 6 sandwiches, toast 12 pieces Potato Bread (page 68) and spread 6 with Horseradish and Mustard and Mayonnaise (page 178). Sauté one bunch julienned mustard greens in butter (page 169). Cook 18 slices Canadian bacon until heated through, about 1 minute per side.

Cover the 6 coated pieces toast with mustard greens, bacon, and thinly sliced tomatoes. Melt 1 tablespoon butter in a large skillet over moderate heat. Fry 6 eggs until yolks are just set, about 1 minute per side. Set each egg atop a plain piece toast. Place egg covered piece on top of tomato to form sandwich. Slice in half and serve with Cole Slaw (page 163), olives, and french fries.

Lamb with Sautéed Eggplant and Onion Marmalade on Naan

Make the Onion Marmalade and let cool.

For 6 sandwiches, marinate ½ pound Bulgarian feta cheese in olive oil (page 232). Slice a medium eggplant in ¼-inch rounds and sauté in ⅔ cup olive oil until golden brown.

Preheat oven to 350°F. Using a serrated knife, slice 6 pieces of Naan (page 69) in half horizontally. Transfer to large baking sheet, cut sides up. Generously spread 6 pieces with Horseradish and Mustard and Mayonnaise (page 178). Cover with eggplant and thinly sliced tomatoes.

Spread remaining 6 pieces with Onion Marmalade. Top with thinly sliced Herb-Stuffed Leg of Lamb (page 79) and crumbled feta cheese. Cover each sandwich half with a damp paper towel. Cook until heated through, about 3 minutes. Remove paper towels and combine the halves to form sandwiches. Cut in half and serve immediately.

Onion Marmalade

½ stick unsalted butter

3 medium onions, thinly sliced

1 teaspoon salt

1 teaspoon freshly ground black pepper

⅓ cup chicken stock

1 teaspoon pureed garlic (page 236)

Melt butter in a large skillet over moderate heat. Add onions, salt, and pepper. Cook until onions are deep, golden brown, stirring occasionally, about 20 minutes. Add garlic, sweat 1 to 2 minutes, then add chicken stock and reduce heat to low. Cook, stirring frequently, about 25 minutes or until mixture is the consistency of marmalade. Set aside to cool to room temperature. (You can make this a day in advance and reserve in refrigerator.)

Roasted Pork with Two Cabbages

For 3 sandwiches, cut a baguette in thirds crosswise, then in half horizontally, or substitute 6 pieces of rye bread. Grill or toast bread in broiler and spread both sides with Horseradish and Mustard and Mayonnaise (page 178). Cover the 3 bottom pieces with a layer of Sweet and Sour Red Cabbage (page 173), then add warm, thinly sliced roasted pork. Cover the 3 top pieces with about ¼ cup Sauerkraut (page 184), cover with slices of Swiss cheese, and broil 2 minutes. Close the bread to form sandwiches. Cut in half and serve.

Skirt Steak on Rye Bread

For 4 sandwiches, toast 8 slices of thickly sliced rye bread and lightly butter. (If the grill is hot, coat the bread with butter and toast on the grill.) Spread about 1½ tablespoons Horseradish and Mustard and Mayonnaise (page 178) on each slice. Cover 4 slices with romaine lettuce, thinly sliced tomatoes, then sliced Marinated Skirt Steak (page 75). Top with remaining toast to form sandwiches. Cut in half and serve with french fries and a watercress salad.

Smoked Chicken Salad and Sweet and Sour Cabbage

For 3 sandwiches, cut a baguette crosswise into thirds, then slice each third in half lengthwise. Pull out about half the doughy center and reserve for another use (i.e., fine dry bread crumbs). Spread stoneground mustard over each piece. Cover 3 pieces of bread with ¾ cup Sweet and Sour Red Cabbage (page 173). Top with Smoked Chicken Salad (page 124), then romaine lettuce. Top with the remaining bread to form sandwiches.

Hot Brisket of Beef Sandwiches

For 6 sandwiches, reheat thinly sliced Beef Brisket (page 77) in its sauce with 6 julienned Dill Pickles (page 186). Cut 2 baguettes in thirds crosswise, then in half horizontally. Arrange bread cut-side up on baking sheet and broil until toasted. Spread generously with Horseradish and Mustard and Mayonnaise (page 178). Place warm meat mixture over 6 slices of bread. Top with thinly sliced tomatoes and green leaf lettuce. Cover with remaining bread. Cut in half and serve warm with Greek Potato Salad (page 151) and Sweet and Sour Red Cabbage (page 173).

Grilled Chicken and Baba Ghanoush

Preheat grill or broiler. For 4 sandwiches, season 4 boneless chicken leg and thigh pieces (with skin) with salt and pepper. Grill about 5 minutes per side. Lightly butter 4 pita breads and toast on grill.

Cut off and discard about 2 inches off top of each pita. Spread ⅓ cup Roasted Eggplant and Sesame (baba ghanoush) (page 156) inside each pita. Slice chicken thinly, across grain. Arrange slices over baba ghanoush and top with thinly sliced tomatoes and romaine lettuce. Serve warm. Can also be served on our homemade buns (page 66).

Breads

Bread baking best captures the essential magic of cooking. It always seems amazing that by simply combining some yeast, flour, and water with a few other ingredients, letting it sit for a while, and applying heat, something as deeply satisfying as bread emerges.

Bread is such an important part of the meal, we suggest you choose it as carefully as the other courses. Here are a few of our specialty breads to get the ideas flowing.

Banana Nut Bread

It takes about 10 minutes to mix this basic quickbread. We like to serve it with a fruit plate and our own Homemade Yogurt (page 181) at lunch. It's also nice at breakfast, spread with cream cheese.

makes 1 loaf

8 tablespoons (1 stick) butter, softened
1 cup granulated sugar
2 large eggs
3 ripe bananas
1 tablespoon milk
1 cup walnuts, coarsely chopped
2 cups all-purpose flour
1 teaspoon salt
1 teaspoon baking soda
1 teaspoon baking powder

Preheat oven to 325°F. Butter a 9 × 5 × 3-inch loaf pan.

Cream butter and sugar until light and fluffy. Add eggs, one at a time, beating well after each addition.

In a small bowl, mash bananas with a fork. Mix in milk and nuts. In another bowl, mix together flour, salt, baking soda, and baking powder.

Add banana mixture to creamed mixture and stir until combined. Add dry ingredients, mixing just until flour disappears.

Pour batter into pan and bake 1 hour to 1 hour 10 minutes, until a toothpick inserted in center comes out clean. Set aside to cool on rack in pan about 15 minutes. Remove from pan, invert, and cool completely on rack.

Hamburger Buns

What could be better than fresh hamburger buns? These freeze well, so you can make the recipe, divide into individual balls, wrap, freeze, and defrost as needed. In addition to salt and pepper, try sprinkling the tops with sesame, poppy, or caraway seeds. And don't limit these lovely buns to vehicles for hamburgers. They're great for holding barbecued beef, sloppy Joes, or plain old tuna salad.

makes 8 to 10 buns

1 cup water

5 tablespoons unsalted butter

2 tablespoons granulated sugar

1½ teaspoons salt

1 tablespoon dry yeast

⅓ cup warm water

1 egg

3½ cups all-purpose flour

1 egg, beaten for wash

coarse salt and cracked black pepper for sprinkling

Bring water to a boil. In a large bowl, combine boiling water with butter, sugar, and salt. Set aside to cool to lukewarm, about 110°F.

Combine yeast and warm water. Stir and set aside until foamy. Add dissolved yeast to water and butter mixture. Add egg and 1 cup flour. Beat at low speed until batter is lump-free. Cover with plastic wrap and set aside in a warm place until doubled and foamy, about 30 minutes.

Add remaining flour and beat until mixture becomes elastic, about 5 minutes. Transfer to buttered plastic container, cover, and refrigerate overnight. Occasionally check dough and punch down.

The next day, divide dough into 9 pieces. Lightly knead each to form a bun and set aside to rest on parchment-lined baking sheet, at room temperature until doubled, ½ hour.

Preheat oven to 375°F. Brush tops with egg wash and sprinkle with salt and pepper. Bake 15 to 20 minutes, until lightly browned. Set aside to cool.

For hamburgers for 6: mix 3 pounds ground beef with 1 onion, diced, and 3 garlic cloves, minced. Divide into 6 patties, sprinkle with salt and pepper, and grill over high heat.

Brioche

For a perfect golden loaf of cakelike bread make sure your eggs and butter are the proper temperature and allow enough time for a long, slow rising. Thanks to its richness, this bread freezes well. We slice it thinly and spread with liver pâté or cream cheese, chives, and smoked fish for canapés. It also makes heavenly toast.

makes 1 loaf

2 teaspoons dry yeast
¼ cup warm water
1 tablespoon granulated sugar
1 teaspoon salt
4 eggs, room temperature
2 cups all-purpose flour
12 tablespoons (1½ sticks) unsalted butter, cool but pliable

Combine yeast and water. Stir to dissolve and set aside.

In a large bowl, stir together sugar, salt, and eggs. Add dissolved yeast mixture and flour. Using an electric mixer, slowly beat about 2 minutes. Increase speed to medium and continue mixing until dough is stringy, about 5 minutes.

With machine running, add butter, a small piece at a time, beating until incorporated. It is important that the butter be the perfect temperature here—not hard, not soft, but sort of plastic-feeling. The dough should be wet and sticky.

Place dough in a buttered bowl, cover with buttered plastic wrap, and set aside in warm place to rise about ½ hour. Punch down, return to bowl, and let rise slowly, in refrigerator, overnight.

On a generously floured board (you may need to flour your fingers—this dough is so sticky), gently knead dough just until a loaf can be formed. Butter a 9 × 5 × 3-inch loaf pan. Place dough in pan, cover with plastic, and set aside in a warm place to rise until doubled, about 45 minutes.

Meanwhile preheat oven to 375°F. Bake 35 to 40 minutes, until bread sounds hollow when tapped. Turn out and cool on a rack.

Potato Bread

A potato gives this wonderful sandwich bread a crumbly, earthy quality and a surprisingly light texture. The recipe comes from the Milliken family's Irish side.

makes 1 loaf

1 baking potato, peeled and cut into large chunks, or 1 cup leftover
   mashed potatoes
1 cup milk
1½ tablespoons lard
1½ tablespoons unsalted butter
1½ teaspoons salt
1 tablespoon granulated sugar
1 tablespoon dry yeast
⅓ cup warm water
5 cups bread flour

Boil potato until soft. Drain and reserve cooking liquid. Rice the potato through a food mill.

Scald milk and combine with ½ cup reserved cooking liquid. Combine liquids and potato with lard, butter, salt, and sugar in a large bowl. Set aside to cool to room temperature.

Meanwhile combine yeast and warm water, and set aside until foamy. When potato mixture has cooled, add yeast mixture. Add flour and knead with a dough hook, on an electric mixer, until smooth and glossy, about 7 minutes.

Transfer to a buttered bowl, cover with plastic wrap, and set aside in warm place to rise about ½ hour. Punch dough down and briefly knead. Butter a 9 × 5 × 3-inch loaf pan. Place dough in pan, cover with plastic, and let rise until doubled, about 45 minutes.

Preheat oven to 350°F. Bake 30 minutes, until bread sounds hollow when tapped.

Naan

Naan—an Indian puffy bread—is traditionally baked on the sides of a red-hot tandoor oven. We've forfeited puffiness and developed a great sour flavor in this adaptation for the American kitchen.

makes 12 individual breads

1 cup warm water, 110°F
1 tablespoon granulated sugar
1 tablespoon dry yeast
1 cup plain yogurt
1 tablespoon salt
4¾ cups bread flour
¼ cup yogurt for spreading
blanched garlic slivers, sautéed diced onion, sesame seeds, or
   coarse salt for garnish

Combine water, sugar and yeast. Set aside until foamy.

In bowl of an electric mixer fitted with a dough hook, combine yogurt, salt, and yeast mixture. With the machine running at medium speed, add flour and knead until smooth and elastic, about 10 minutes.

Coat a bowl with butter. Transfer kneaded dough to bowl, cover with plastic wrap, and set aside to rise at room temperature, about 45 minutes.

Coat a sheet pan with vegetable oil. Punch down dough and divide into 12 equal pieces. Knead each by hand to form a roll and place on baking sheet. Cover with oiled parchment paper or plastic wrap and set aside to rise until doubled, about 15 minutes.

Preheat oven to 550°F.

Stretch each piece (or roll with a pin) to form a 5-inch long oblong. Let rise an additional 5 minutes. Before baking, transfer to a dry sheet pan. Spread a teaspoon yogurt in center of each and sprinkle with garlic, onion, or other toppings. Bake about 12 minutes, until golden.

4 Entrées

Beef, Lamb, Pork, Veal, and Other Meats

If there is a common theme to our meat entrées, it is the uncommon cut of meat. Our hearts inevitably go out to the neglected and often inexpensive cuts like lamb shank, pork shoulder, beef short ribs, and veal breast. While it takes more time and effort to cook them, they deliver the deep flavors and gaminess we look for in meats.

A great advantage to using unusual cuts is that they allow us to offer our guests something they don't ordinarily cook at home, and in ample portions. Organ meats, like liver and kidney, are a great bargain. Properly cleaned of tendons (you can ask the butcher to do this) and cooked quickly, they can be as luxurious as the finest tenderloin, at one-quarter the price. We hope you'll give them a try.

Marinated Beef Short Ribs

Thin beef short ribs are first roasted and basted to break down tough tendons, then marinated in a delicious Oriental barbecue sauce before a quick trip to the grill. We love to eat them in combination with Spicy Cold Soba Noodles (page 143) and Chopped Tofu with Parsley salad (page 135).

The key to this popular dish lies in the correct cut of short ribs. Ask a butcher to cut from the short plate, flanken style. The ribs should be cut across the bones in half-inch slices, leaving not a single rib, but a small cross section of about four ribs in each piece.

6 servings

3¾ pounds beef short ribs, cut in ½-inch slices with bones

salt and freshly ground black pepper to taste

½ cup water

2 tablespoons fresh lemon juice

1 teaspoon dried red pepper flakes

MARINADE

¼ cup hoisin sauce (page 234)

3 tablespoons plum sauce (page 234)

2 tablespoons oyster sauce (page 234)

2 tablespoons soy sauce

1 tablespoon peanut oil

1 tablespoon sesame oil

1 tablespoon honey

1 tablespoon chili paste (page 233)

1 tablespoon pureed garlic (page 235)

1 tablespoon freshly grated ginger (page 235)

1 bunch cilantro, stems trimmed and roughly chopped

1 bunch scallions, finely chopped

Preheat oven to 350°F.

Season ribs with salt and pepper. Lay across a rack in a roasting pan or baking sheet and bake 10 minutes. In a small bowl, combine water, lemon juice, and red pepper flakes. Brush over top side of ribs and bake an additional 10 minutes. Turn, brush again, and bake 10 minutes more. Set aside to cool.

Combine marinade ingredients in a large bowl. Add roasted ribs and toss to coat. Cover with plastic wrap and refrigerate a minimum of 4 hours or as long as 24.

Preheat grill or broiler. Grill for 2 minutes per side and serve immediately with Spicy Cold Soba Noodles (page 143) and Chopped Tofu with Parsley (page 135).

Grilled Pepper Steak with Tamarind Chutney

Chutneys are often used in India, instead of elaborate sauces, to cool down a hot taste. In this barbecued dish, tart tamarind supplies the perfect complement to the steak's hot peppery crust. If you prefer a less spicy steak and more aromatic flavors, mix equal parts celery seed, cracked black peppercorns, mustard seeds, and sesame seeds. Rib eye is fattier than sirloin, but in our eyes much more flavorful.

6 servings

If tamarind is not available, a sweet mango chutney would be good.

makes ¾ cup

6 (12-ounce) beef rib eye or sirloin steaks
½ cup cracked black peppercorns (page 235)
salt to taste
Tamarind Chutney, recipe follows

Preheat heavy-bottomed pan. Coat steaks generously on both sides with cracked peppercorns and sprinkle with salt. Sauté steaks, being careful not to burn the pepper, about 8 minutes per side, for medium rare. (We like to sear the edges of steak to brown the fat, thereby releasing more flavor.)

Spread a thin layer Tamarind Chutney on 6 serving plates. Place steaks on top and serve remaining chutney in ramekins.

Tamarind Chutney

1 pound dry tamarind (page 235) or ½ cup pulp
2½ teaspoons brown sugar
2 teaspoons freshly grated ginger (page 235)
¼ teaspoon salt
dash of freshly ground black pepper

If using dry tamarind, extract pulp by first removing the hard outer pods. Place fruit in a medium saucepan and add enough water to cover. Bring to a boil and cook, uncovered, until flesh is soft, about 20 minutes. Push through a strainer and discard any seeds or bits of shell.

Combine pulp in a bowl with remaining ingredients. Chutney may be kept in refrigerator up to 5 days.

Marinated Skirt Steak with Horseradish Mustard

You can't go wrong with skirt steak for informal outdoor gatherings. This inexpensive, well-marbled cut benefits from long marination and cooking over high heat. Just slice it thin and serve with simple accompaniments like baked potatoes or grilled corn and beer.

6 servings

3 pounds skirt steak

1 cup olive oil

2 tablespoons red wine vinegar

½ cup soy sauce

2 teaspoons pureed garlic (page 236)

2 teaspoons dry mustard

2 teaspoons Worcestershire sauce

1 teaspoon Tabasco

1 teaspoon cracked black pepper (page 235)

Horseradish Mustard for garnish, recipe follows

Trim steak of any outer pieces of fat or silver skin. Marbling within beef should remain. Combine remaining ingredients in a bowl. Place steak in a medium glass or ceramic roasting pan and add marinade, making sure beef is entirely covered. Cover with plastic wrap and refrigerate a minimum of 8 hours or as long as 2 days.

When marinated, grill or sauté meat. If grilling, a very hot, high fire is best. (We prefer hardwood charcoal like mesquite, oak, or cherry.) Grill 2 minutes per side for rare. Or sear in a sauté pan, 2 minutes per side, in 2 tablespoons vegetable oil over high heat.

To serve, slice thinly, at an angle, across grain. Fan slices on serving plates and add small mounds of Fried Onions (page 85), Sweet and Sour Red Cabbage (page 173), and Horseradish Mustard.

Horseradish Mustard

1 cup stoneground mustard

¾ cup freshly grated or jarred white horseradish

makes 1¾ cups

Mix and serve with Marinated Skirt Steak.

Marinated Rib Eye with Gorgonzola Sauce

This hearty marinade marries well with the strong taste of beef and fragrant Gorgonzola and Madeira in the sauce. Serve along with our thin Roasted Potatoes (page 145) to meat and potato lovers.

4 servings

4 (10-ounce) beef rib eye or sirloin steaks

MARINADE

1 cup olive oil

2 tablespoons dry mustard

1 tablespoon Worcestershire sauce

1 teaspoon minced garlic

1 teaspoon soy sauce

1 teaspoon fresh lemon juice

dash of Tabasco

salt and freshly ground black pepper to taste

GORGONZOLA SAUCE

4 tablespoons (½ stick) unsalted butter, cold

6 shallots, finely diced

⅔ cup Madeira

1½ cups Brown Veal Stock (page 57)

4 to 6 ounces (½ to ¾ cup) Gorgonzola cheese, crumbled

Trim steaks of all fat. Combine marinade ingredients in a large container. Add steaks, cover, and refrigerate 6 to 24 hours. Remove meat from refrigerator 2 hours before serving to enhance flavors.

Preheat grill or broiler. Melt 2 tablespoons butter in a medium skillet or saucepan over medium-high heat. Sauté shallots until brown. Add Madeira and cook until wine is reduced by half. Add Brown Veal Stock and reduce again by half. Reduce heat to moderate. Break remaining butter into small pieces and whisk into sauce until smooth. Whisk in crumbled cheese and remove from heat.

Grill or broil steaks 5 minutes per side for medium-rare. Place on warm serving plates, top with sauce, and serve immediately.

Beef Brisket

Brisket is easy to cook and great to have on hand for a comforting winter meal. It reheats beautifully for sandwiches or weeknight suppers with Mashed Potatoes (page 155) or potato pancakes and homemade Applesauce (page 185). If you prefer a thinner sauce, just ladle the broth over the sliced meat and chopped vegetables.

6 servings

3½ pounds beef brisket

4 tablespoons paprika

2 teaspoons salt

1 teaspoon freshly ground black pepper

¼ cup all-purpose flour

½ cup vegetable oil or chicken fat

2 medium onions, sliced

4 carrots, peeled and sliced

2 celery stalks, sliced

2 tablespoons tomato paste

3 bay leaves

1 teaspoon dried thyme

½ teaspoon cracked black pepper (page 235)

salt to taste

3 quarts water

Preheat oven to 350°F. Sprinkle meat generously with paprika, salt, and pepper. Spread flour on a large platter and dip brisket to evenly coat.

Heat oil in a large Dutch oven over high heat. Brown meat on all sides until crusty. Remove from pan and reserve. Add onions, carrots, and celery, and cook until golden, about 5 minutes. Add tomato paste and cook 2 minutes. Add remaining ingredients and meat, and bring to a boil. Cover and transfer to oven. Bake 1 hour on each side or until the meat slips easily off a fork.

Transfer meat to cutting board and set aside 10 minutes before slicing. Carefully skim and discard fat from cooking liquid in pot. Discard bay leaves. Puree remaining sauce and vegetables in a blender. Strain through a sieve. Taste and adjust seasonings. Slice meat thinly across grain, top with warm sauce, and serve immediately.

Beef Stroganoff

Our updated Beef Stroganoff is easy and elegant—great for company. By using beef tenderloin to make this old favorite, preparation time has been cut dramatically. The simple creamed sauce can be made ahead and reheated while you prepare the noodles and sear the beef.

6 servings

2½ pounds beef tenderloin, trimmed
1 tablespoon unsalted butter
2½ cups sliced mushroom caps
¼ teaspoon salt
dash of pepper
1½ cups dill pickles julienned, with 2 tablespoons pickle juice
2 cups heavy cream
salt and freshly ground black pepper to taste
2 tablespoons vegetable oil

Remove any silver skin surrounding tenderloin and cut into 1-inch slices, across width. Slightly flatten slices by pressing with the palm of your hand. Set aside.

Melt butter in a medium skillet over medium-high heat. Sauté mushrooms with salt and pepper until golden, about 5 minutes. Add pickles and juice, and cook until juice evaporates slightly, about 2 minutes. Add cream and cook until reduced by half. While sauce is reducing, cook beef.

Season meat sparingly with salt and pepper, since sauce will be salty from the pickles. Heat a heavy large skillet over high heat, add oil and heat until it starts smoking. Sear meat briefly, 2 minutes per side for medium-rare. Serve beef over a bed of homemade fettuccine, with warm sauce ladled over all.

Herb-Stuffed Leg of Lamb
with Pimento Sauce

By removing the center bone, leg of lamb is much easier to carve and serve to guests. Feel free to increase the amount of garlic and herbs to taste; this strongly flavored meat is enhanced by assertive seasonings.

6 servings

1 (6-pound) boneless leg of lamb, with shank
salt and freshly ground black pepper to taste
3 tablespoons pureed garlic (page 236)
½ cup assorted chopped fresh herbs, such as parsley, oregano,
   basil, thyme, chives, mint
2 tablespoons olive oil
Pimento Sauce, recipe follows

Ask a butcher to remove all bones, except shank, and to clean meat of all sinew and excess fat inside and out. Butterfly leg for stuffing.

Preheat oven to 375°F. Lay lamb flat on counter. Using a sharp knife, make several slits, about 2 inches long by ¼ inch deep, so seasonings can penetrate meat. Sprinkle generously with salt and pepper. Spread garlic evenly on top, then cover with herbs. Roll meat to enclose stuffing and tie with string at 1-inch intervals, keeping the diameter of the roll the same so that the roast cooks evenly. Shank bone will protrude at one end. Generously season outside with salt and pepper.

Heat oil in a large skillet over high heat. Brown lamb on all sides. Roast on rack in roasting pan 30 to 40 minutes for medium-rare, 1 hour for well done. (A meat thermometer inserted in center should read 160 to 165°F or a thin-bladed knife inserted to the center for 20 seconds should feel lukewarm on your lips.) Let sit at room temperature about 10 minutes before carving, so juices can run to center. Remove strings and slice meat thinly across the roll. Top with Pimento Sauce and serve with a side dish of City Ratatouille (page 176). To reheat carved lamb, place slices on a sheet pan, cover with a wet towel, and bake 5 minutes at 375°F.

Use leftovers for sandwiches (pages 60 to 63).

(continued)

Pimento Sauce

2 tablespoons olive oil

5 shallots, finely sliced

½ cup mushrooms, sliced

¾ cup dry white wine

5 cups Brown Lamb Stock (page 57) or canned beef broth

1 teaspoon tomato paste

3 tablespoons pimento or roasted red pepper pureed in blender
   (with lamb stock if necessary)

1 teaspoon pureed garlic (page 236)

1 tablespoon unsalted butter, cold

salt and freshly ground black pepper to taste

Heat oil in a medium saucepan over moderate heat. Cook shallots and mushrooms until golden. Add wine, turn heat to high, and reduce by half. Add Brown Lamb Stock and reduce again by a quarter. Whisk in tomato paste, pimento puree, and garlic. Break butter into small pieces and whisk into sauce until smooth. Adjust seasonings and strain through a fine sieve. Serve warm with sliced, roasted lamb or Moussaka (recipe follows).

Moussaka

We have lightened this traditional Greek dish by reducing the custard and eggplant, and adding extra ground lamb and a layer of julienned vegetables. Moussaka is terrific for large crowds since it can be prepared in advance and reheated without any loss of quality.

10 to 12 servings

MEAT FILLING

2 tablespoons olive oil

1 large onion, diced

2 pounds ground lamb (leftover lamb can be ground and used)

2 tablespoons pureed garlic (page 236)

4 tomatoes, peeled, seeded, and diced (page 236)

½ cup brandy

½ cup tarragon vinegar

2 tablespoons ground cumin

1 tablespoon salt

½ teaspoon freshly ground black pepper

Preheat oven to 400°F. Heat oil in a large ovenproof skillet over moderate heat. Cook onions until soft. Add lamb and garlic, and cook until browned, stirring occasionally. When meat is well-browned, stir in remaining ingredients. Transfer to oven and bake until quite dry, about 45 minutes. Set aside to cool.

EGGPLANT

3 large eggplants, with skins

coarse salt

2 cups olive oil

Cut eggplants into ¼-inch slices, lengthwise. Sprinkle with salt on both sides and let rest on a rack until moisture rises to surface, about 30 minutes. Pat dry with paper towels. Heat oil in a large skillet over medium-high heat. Fry eggplant briefly, 1 to 2 minutes per side. Set aside to drain on paper towels.

(continued)

VEGETABLE FILLING

3 carrots, peeled and thinly sliced
1 cup (4 ounces) Chinese snow peas
2 leeks, white and light green parts, cut in half
3 celery stalks, peeled and cut into 1-inch lengths
2 cups mushroom caps
4 tablespoons (½ stick) unsalted butter
½ teaspoon salt

Wash and dry all vegetables, then cut into fine julienne. Blanch carrots and peas in a small saucepan of salted boiling water just until water returns to a boil. Refresh in cold water, drain, and reserve.

Melt butter in a medium skillet over moderate heat. Cook leeks along with salt 1 minute, add celery and cook 1 minute, then mushrooms and cook an additional minute. Set aside to cool. Toss all vegetables together in a large bowl and reserve.

CUSTARD

9 eggs
2¼ cups heavy cream
1¼ teaspoons salt
¼ teaspoon freshly ground black pepper
¼ teaspoon freshly grated nutmeg
¾ cup grated Parmesan cheese

Combine eggs, cream, salt, pepper, and nutmeg in a bowl. Whisk until smooth. Pass through a strainer to remove any stray eggshells. Whisk in Parmesan cheese and set aside.

1 recipe Pimento Sauce (page 80)

To assemble: Preheat oven to 350°F. Stir one-third custard into meat filling. Combine remaining custard with vegetable filling.

In a 9 × 13-inch roasting pan or casserole, arrange one-third eggplant slices to completely cover bottom. (The slices may overlap. That's fine.) Spread half meat filling on top, then cover with another third eggplant. Pour all vegetables in custard on top. Cover with remaining eggplant, then spread remaining meat mixture evenly over top.

Place pan inside a larger roasting pan and pour boiling water into roasting pan until it rises halfway up the sides of the moussaka pan. Bake, uncovered, until custard is set in center, about 1½ hours. You can test for doneness by sticking a knife in center, then pressing area around knife. If custard oozes out, cook longer.

Cut into individual portions and lift out with a spatula. Serve immediately, topped with Pimento Sauce. Moussaka can be made 1 or 2 days in advance and reheated in a 325°F oven 25 minutes.

Braised Lamb Shanks with Oregano and Feta

Inexpensive cuts like the shank take longer to cook, but the resulting flavors are deeper and more satisfying than more expensive cuts. In this Greek peasant dish—similar to ossobuco—the meat flakes off the bone into a delicious tomato and herb broth.

6 servings

6 lamb shanks, trimmed of excess fat
salt and freshly ground black pepper, to taste
1 cup all-purpose flour
1 cup vegetable oil
3 medium onions, thinly sliced
3 quarts Brown Lamb Stock (page 57) or canned chicken broth
4 bunches oregano, stems and leaves separated, leaves chopped
¼ teaspoon cayenne pepper
2 large tomatoes, peeled, seeded, and diced (page 236)
1 cup feta cheese, crumbled

Generously sprinkle shanks with salt and pepper, then dip in flour to lightly coat. Heat oil in a large Dutch oven over high heat. Brown shanks on all sides, transfer to a platter, and reserve.

Reduce heat to medium and cook onions in same pan, stirring occasionally, until golden brown. Return shanks to pan. Add Brown Lamb Stock, all oregano stems, half oregano leaves, and cayenne. (If shanks are not completely covered by liquid, add enough water to cover.) Bring to a boil, reduce to a simmer, and cook, covered, about 1½ hours, occasionally skimming foam and fat that rise to top. To test for doneness, pierce with a fork. If shank slides easily off fork, meat is tender. Remove from heat.

Using a slotted spoon and a fork, lift out lamb shanks. Cover with a damp towel and set aside in a warm place. Pass sauce through a fine sieve into a medium saucepan, pressing with a ladle to extract all juices. Skim fat from top and bring sauce to a boil. Stir in tomatoes and remaining oregano, and remove from heat.

To serve, arrange a shank on top of a bed of bulgur wheat (page 233) in each serving bowl. Sprinkle feta cheese evenly over each shank, add sauce, and serve immediately.

Lamb Curry with Fried Onions

The key to a satisfying stew—and a curry is really just a spicy stew—is starting with large chunks of meat. The small pieces labeled as stewing meat in the supermarket become smaller and tougher as the stew bubbles on top of the stove. So please, start big!

6 servings

4 pounds boneless, trimmed lamb shoulder
salt and freshly ground black pepper to taste
1 cup vegetable oil
3 medium onions, diced
2 tablespoons pureed garlic (page 236)
2 tablespoons black mustard seeds (page 232)
2 tablespoons garam masala (page 233)
2 teaspoons turmeric
2 teaspoons ground cardamom
2 teaspoons ground cumin
1 teaspoon dried red pepper flakes
2 quarts Brown Lamb Stock (page 57) or canned chicken broth
plain yogurt and Fried Onions, recipe follows, for garnish

Cut meat, as uniformly as possible, into 2 × 3-inch cubes. Generously sprinkle with salt and pepper.

Heat oil in a large Dutch oven over high heat. Cook meat until golden brown on all sides, then reserve on a platter. In same pot, cook onions, stirring occasionally, until golden. Reduce heat to medium, add garlic and all dry spices, and cook about 3 minutes, stirring constantly. Return meat to pan and pour in Brown Lamb Stock. Bring to a boil, reduce to a simmer, and cook, uncovered, 1 hour 15 minutes. Occasionally skim and discard fat that rises to top.

Ladle warm stew over a bed of Basmati Rice (page 146) and serve with Orange Dal with Ginger and Garlic (page 136). Garnish with yogurt and Fried Onions, and serve immediately.

Fried Onions

1 large onion
¼ cup vegetable oil

(continued)

Peel onion and slice as thinly as possible, more like a shave than a cut, across width. (You may need to use a meat slicer or food processor fitted with a 1-millimeter blade to slice it this fine.)

Heat oil over moderate heat in a small skillet. Working in small batches, fry onions, constantly shaking the pan, just until crispy and golden, about 3 minutes. Remove onions with tongs or a slotted spoon and drain on paper towels.

6 servings

Barbecued Baby Back Ribs

These are the messiest, juiciest, most delicious ribs ever. Serve with bowls of barbecue sauce for dipping. Our favorite accompaniments are mashed potatoes, applesauce, grilled corn on the cob, and plenty of cold beer, of course. Leftover barbecue sauce, perfect for brushing over chicken, will keep about a week.

6 to 8 servings

2 quarts water

1 cup vinegar

½ cup fresh lemon juice

1 tablespoon dried red pepper flakes

⅛ cup salt

½ teaspoon paprika

6 (12-rib) racks baby back ribs

BARBECUE SAUCE

12 dry ancho chiles (page 232)

1 cup vinegar

3 cups water

¼ cup vegetable oil

3 onions, diced

1½ tablespoons pureed garlic (page 235)

1½ tablespoons ground cumin

3 cups chicken stock or canned broth

¼ cup plus 2 tablespoons packed brown sugar

¼ cup fresh orange juice

¼ cup fresh lemon or lime juice

¼ cup ketchup

Preheat oven to 350°F. Combine first 6 ingredients in a large roasting pan. Add ribs and marinate ½ hour.

Arrange ribs on rack in roasting pan, standing up if possible. Bake 2 hours, brushing every 20 minutes with water and vinegar marinade.

Meanwhile, make Barbecue Sauce. Split open chiles and remove seeds. Lightly roast over open flame or under broiler until brown and puffy, not black. Combine vinegar and water in a large bowl, add roasted chiles, and marinate about 2 hours. Transfer chiles and liquid to a food processor and puree until smooth, then strain.

Heat oil in a large skillet over medium-high heat. Sauté onions until brown. Add garlic and cumin and sauté a moment, then add pureed chiles and chicken stock. Reduce to a simmer and cook 40 to 60 minutes.

Preheat grill or broiler to low. Combine remaining ingredients in a small bowl and make a paste. Whisk into sauce and cook an additional 15 minutes. Taste and adjust seasonings.

Dip roasted rib racks into Barbecue Sauce. Grill until warmed through and glazed, about 4 to 8 minutes per side.

Grilled Veal Chops with Thyme Vinaigrette

This easy entrée captures the essence of good summer entertaining—just a cool sauce over simply grilled meat. The key to cooking veal outside is to let the grill cool down to a low, even fire and then almost roast, rather than sear, the meat.

6 servings

6 (1-inch-thick) veal chops
salt and freshly ground pepper to taste
½ bunch fresh thyme, leaves only, chopped
2 shallots, finely diced
⅓ cup extra virgin olive oil
juice of 1 small lemon

Preheat grill or broiler. Season chops to taste with salt and pepper. When coals have cooled down, grill 8 to 10 minutes per side.

Meanwhile combine remaining ingredients in a small bowl to make a vinaigrette. Taste and adjust seasonings, and spoon over warm chops. Serve immediately.

Veal Kidneys with Lemon and Soy

This smooth, rich meat has the most luxurious texture imaginable. Serve over a bed of crisp Fried Spinach (page 158) for just the right contrast.

6 servings

6 (6-ounce) veal kidneys
salt and freshly ground black pepper to taste
¾ cup fine dry bread crumbs
6 tablespoons (¾ stick) unsalted butter for sautéing
2 tablespoons soy sauce
2 tablespoons fresh lemon juice
6 tablespoons Brown Veal Stock (page 57) or chicken stock
8 tablespoons (1 stick) unsalted butter, cold

Trim kidneys of all visible fat and sinew. Cut into ¾-inch horizontal slices, at an angle. Sprinkle with salt and pepper, then coat with bread crumbs.

Melt butter for sautéing in a large skillet over medium-high heat. Sauté kidneys until golden brown on each side, about 2 minutes per side. Transfer to a platter and set aside in a warm place.

In the same pan, combine soy sauce and lemon juice, and cook over moderate heat until slightly reduced. Pour in Brown Veal Stock and reduce by half. Break cold butter into small pieces and whisk into sauce until smooth. Pour any blood or juice that has drained from kidneys into sauce and mix.

Arrange kidneys on a bed of Fried Spinach (page 158) and spoon over sauce. Serve immediately.

Calf's Liver with Port Wine and Ginger

This sweet, strong sauce stands up well to the distinctive flavor of liver. It is best to make the sauce first, and keep it warm or reheat it while quickly cooking the meat. Most "bad" liver is simply overcooked.

6 servings

PORT SAUCE

10 tablespoons (1 stick plus 2 tablespoons) unsalted butter, cold
6 tablespoons minced shallots
¾ teaspoon salt
2 heaping tablespoons freshly grated ginger (page 235)
1¼ cups red port
1½ cups Brown Veal Stock (page 57) or canned broth
1 cup heavy cream
6 tablespoons clarified butter (page 235) for frying (optional)
6 (8-ounce) slices calf's liver, trimmed of all sinew and cut into
    ½-inch slices
salt and freshly ground black pepper to taste

To make sauce, melt 2 tablespoons butter in a medium skillet over moderate heat. Sauté shallots with salt until golden. Add ginger and cook briefly, stirring occasionally, until aroma is released.

Remove from heat and add port. Cook over high heat until reduced by half. Add Brown Veal Stock, reduce again by half, then add cream. Bring to a boil and add remaining butter, broken in small pieces. Whisk sauce until smooth and remove from heat. Strain to remove any "hairs" from ginger.

Preheat grill or heat clarified butter in a large skillet over high heat. Season liver with salt and pepper, and cook briefly, about 3 minutes per side. Serve immediately over Fried Onions (page 85) with Port Sauce spooned on top.

Poultry

While chicken may be the most accommodating main course ingredient—even those on restricted diets can usually eat it—the challenge for the adventurous cook is how to avoid kitchen boredom. How many times can you grill a plain chicken breast? With that in mind, we've tried to select recipes with an eye toward ethnic diversity: There's a tropical duck curry from Thailand, a stuffed turkey breast from Italy, French duck confit, and a homey Mediterranean chicken in tomato and vegetable broth, to name just a few.

We suggest you explore the wide variety of types and cuts of poultry now available in your local supermarket. Boneless chicken thighs, for example, are great for grilling. They don't dry out as easily as the more expensive breasts and their dark meat is much more flavorful. Turkey is another great buy. The breast meat, available boned and even sliced, is fat-free and can be used as a substitute for costly veal escalopes in quick sautés and grilled dishes. As for duck, that most luxurious bird, we've worked at reducing the amount of fat on the plate.

Rigatoni Stuffed with Chicken and Fennel

¾ pound rigatoni

1 tablespoon olive oil

¾ pound ground chicken, white meat only

1 tablespoon fennel seeds, roughly chopped

1 egg white

1¼ cups heavy cream, cold

1 teaspoon salt

½ teaspoon freshly ground black pepper

2 dashes of Tabasco

CREAM SAUCE

2½ cups heavy cream

½ cup freshly grated Parmesan cheese

1 teaspoon salt

½ teaspoon freshly ground black pepper

2 tablespoons chopped fresh chives for garnish

Cook rigatoni in a large pot of rapidly boiling salted water until al dente, about 8 minutes. Drain in a colander and chill in a large bowl of iced water. Drain chilled pasta until nearly dry and toss with olive oil to coat. Reserve.

Puree chicken, fennel, and egg white in a food processor until smooth, about 2 minutes. Transfer to a bowl nested inside a larger bowl half-filled with iced water. Stir until evenly chilled.

Add cream, a quarter cup at a time, stirring vigorously with a wooden spoon after each addition, until all is added. Stir in salt, pepper, and Tabasco. (At this stage, the stuffing can be stored in refrigerator up to 24 hours.)

To stuff rigatoni, fill a pastry bag fitted with a #4 plain tip with chicken mixture and stuff rigatoni from both ends. Reserve.

Preheat oven to 400°F.

To make sauce, combine cream, Parmesan cheese, salt, and pepper in a medium ovenproof skillet. Bring to a boil. Add stuffed rigatoni, return to a boil, then transfer to oven. Bake until sauce is thick and bubbly, and rigatoni is cooked through, about 10 minutes.

Spoon into serving bowls or plates, sprinkle with chives, and serve hot.

Chicken Stuffed with Cilantro and Turmeric

Turmeric and cilantro lend a distinctive Indian flavor and brilliant golden color to roasted chicken. This is a wonderful stuffing to try with Cornish hens or other small birds like poussin.

6 servings

6 boneless chicken legs and thighs, with skin
3 boneless whole chicken breasts, with skin
salt and freshly ground black pepper to taste
4 teaspoons turmeric
¼ cup olive oil
3 bunches cilantro, stems trimmed and roughly chopped
Fresh Tomato Sauce, recipe follows

Preheat oven to 400°F.

Run your fingers between the skin and meat of each piece of chicken, leaving one side attached, to create a pocket for stuffing. Season all over with salt and pepper.

Combine turmeric, 2 tablespoons olive oil, and cilantro in a small bowl to form a paste. Divide into 9 equal parts and spread evenly between skin and meat.

Heat remaining olive oil in a large ovenproof skillet over medium-high heat. Fry chicken, skin-side down first, until golden brown, about 2 minutes per side. Transfer to oven and bake 15 minutes.

Serve immediately, over a bed of bulgur wheat (page 233) or rice, with Fresh Tomato Sauce spooned on top.

(*continued*)

Fresh Tomato Sauce

10 tablespoons (1 stick plus 2 tablespoons) unsalted butter, cold
6 shallots, minced
3 cups peeled, seeded, and diced tomatoes (page 236)
¾ teaspoon salt
¼ teaspoon freshly ground black pepper
1 teaspoon fresh lemon juice
3 tablespoons chopped fresh parsley

Melt 2 tablespoons butter in a medium sauté pan over moderate heat. Cook shallots just until golden. Add tomatoes, salt, and pepper, and cook an additional 3 minutes, uncovered. Break remaining butter into tablespoon-sized pieces and stir in, along with lemon juice. When smooth, remove from heat, stir in parsley, and serve.

makes 4 cups

Chicken Breast with Garlic and Parsley

3 heads garlic, peeled and thinly sliced
6 boneless, whole chicken breasts, with skin
salt and freshly ground black pepper to taste
2 bunches Italian parsley, stems trimmed and roughly chopped
3 tablespoons rendered chicken fat (page 236) or vegetable oil
Cool Tomato Puree, recipe follows

Preheat oven to 400°F. Blanch garlic in a small pot of rapidly boiling, salted water for 1 minute. Drain and set aside to cool.

Create a pocket for stuffing by running your fingers between the skin and meat of each breast, leaving one side attached. Season all over with salt and pepper.

Our favorite technique for stuffing chicken is to place the flavorings between skin and meat, so that every bite is infused with flavor. This simple garlic and parsley combination is just right in the summertime, especially with the added punch of the cool sauce. Plan in advance, since the Tomato Puree must be chilled before serving.

6 servings

In a small bowl, combine chopped parsley and garlic. Divide into 6 equal parts and stuff each breast between skin and meat, spreading evenly.

Heat chicken fat or oil in a large ovenproof skillet over medium-high heat. Sauté chicken, skin-side down first, until golden brown, about 2 minutes per side. Transfer to oven and bake about 10 minutes. Set aside for 5 minutes, to redistribute juices before serving.

Whisk Cool Tomato Puree and coat 6 serving plates with it. Cut each breast into ½-inch slices, across the width. Arrange slices over puree and serve.

Cool Tomato Puree

> 7 medium, ripe tomatoes
> ⅔ cup extra virgin olive oil
> 1 teaspoon salt
> ¼ teaspoon freshly ground black pepper

Core tomatoes, cut in half horizontally, and remove seeds. Puree half the tomatoes in a blender until liquefied, then add olive oil, salt, and pepper. Puree until smooth. (Thin with a few tablespoons water if sauce seems thick.) Strain to remove any seeds and chill until serving time. Puree can be made a day in advance. Whisk before serving.

makes 3 cups

Grilled Chicken with Roasted Peppers

With their moist, dark meat, chicken legs can withstand the high heat of the grill without sacrificing flavor or texture. In this colorful summer dish, grilled chicken legs are awash in a lively tomato and bell pepper broth.

6 servings

6 whole chicken legs with thighs

salt and freshly ground black pepper to taste

3 tablespoons olive oil for brushing

3 tablespoons unsalted butter

2 medium onions, thinly sliced

1 teaspoon salt

1 teaspoon freshly ground black pepper

2 garlic cloves, minced

1 teaspoon paprika

2 each red, green, and yellow peppers roasted, peeled, seeded, and julienned (page 236)

1 tomato, peeled, seeded, and julienned (page 236)

1¼ cups chicken stock or canned broth

Preheat grill or broiler. Season chicken to taste with salt and pepper, and lightly brush with olive oil. Grill or broil, skin-side down first, about 10 minutes per side. (To mark skin with a crisscross pattern, begin cooking on the grill's hottest area until marks appear, then finish on the cooler area to avoid drying out meat.)

Melt butter in a medium skillet over medium-high heat. Cook onions with salt and pepper until soft and clear. Add garlic and paprika, and cook an additional minute, stirring constantly. Add remaining ingredients, bring to a boil, reduce to a simmer, and cook, uncovered, about 5 minutes.

Place chicken over individual beds of bulgur wheat (page 233), rice, or pasta. Ladle on sauce and serve immediately.

Spicy City Chicken

True Indian cooking is much more complex and subtle than the fiery-hot westernized versions served in America. This fragrant chicken dish is sweet, sour, and spicy—all at once.

6 servings

3 pounds boneless chicken breasts and thighs
salt and freshly ground black pepper to taste
2 tablespoons vegetable oil
1 tablespoon fresh lime juice
6 scallions
2 tablespoons unsalted butter
6 shallots, diced
6 large mushrooms, thinly sliced
1 bunch cilantro, stems and leaves separated
1½ jalapeño peppers, chopped with seeds
2 tablespoons ground cumin
2 cups chicken stock or canned broth
1 cup heavy cream
3 egg yolks
3 tablespoons palm sugar (page 234) or brown sugar
¼ cup red wine vinegar

Preheat broiler or prepare grill. Season chicken lightly with salt and pepper, since sauce will be spicy. Mix oil and lime juice in a small bowl and brush chicken and scallions with it.

Broil or grill thighs about 12 minutes, breasts about 9 minutes, and scallions about 2 minutes per side. Always grill chicken skin-side down first.

Meanwhile, make sauce by melting butter in a medium skillet over moderate heat. Cook shallots and mushrooms until soft and golden, about 10 minutes. Add cilantro stems, jalapeño peppers, and cumin, lower heat, and cook for 5 minutes. Add chicken stock. Turn heat to high and cook until liquid is reduced by half. Add cream and return to a boil. Remove from heat. Puree in a blender, strain, and return to heat.

Whisk egg yolks, sugar, and vinegar together in a small bowl.

(*continued*)

Pour one cup pureed sauce into egg mixture to temper. Then combine egg mixture and puree and cook over low heat, stirring constantly, until sauce is thick and smooth.

Arrange grilled chicken over a bed of Basmati Rice (page 146) and spoon sauce over all. Garnish with cilantro leaves and scallions, and serve immediately.

Paupiette of Turkey

These rich little turkey rolls are bursting with the flavors of Italy. It's best to stuff the turkey in advance to firmly set the filling and reduce last-minute preparation. The browned butter sauce is a snap.

6 servings

2 tablespoons olive oil
2 bunches spinach, washed and dried
salt and freshly ground black pepper to taste
1 (2½-pound) skinless, boneless turkey breast
6 slices prosciutto, cut in quarters
1 cup freshly grated Gruyère or Parmesan cheese
1 cup all-purpose flour
4 eggs, lightly beaten
2 cups fine dry bread crumbs
10 tablespoons (1 stick plus 2 tablespoons) unsalted
   butter, cold
1 tablespoon fresh lemon juice
2 tablespoons chopped fresh parsley
½ teaspoon salt
½ teaspoon freshly ground black pepper

Heat olive oil in a large sauté pan over medium-high heat. Cook spinach with salt and pepper just until wilted, about 2 minutes. Set spinach in refrigerator to cool.

Carefully trim turkey of any tendons or cartilage. Slice across grain into ½-inch scallops. Place between 2 layers plastic wrap and flatten by pressing with flat side of a mallet until scallops are ¼ inch thick.

Arrange turkey on a counter and cover each scallop with a layer prosciutto and grated cheese. Squeeze moisture out of spinach, divide, and place evenly over cheese. Roll each to form a small, tight cylinder, enclosing filling.

Dip each roll in flour, patting off any excess. Then dip in eggs, drain, and coat with bread crumbs. Dip again in eggs and bread crumbs. Reserve in refrigerator at least ½ hour to set, or as long as 12 hours.

Preheat oven to 350°F. Melt 5 tablespoons butter in a large ovenproof skillet over medium-high heat. Sauté chilled turkey rolls until golden on all sides. Transfer to oven and bake for 15 minutes, until cheese begins to ooze.

Meanwhile, melt remaining butter in a medium skillet over medium-high heat, shaking pan occasionally to avoid browning. When butter is golden and foamy, about 5 minutes, remove from heat. Stir in lemon juice, parsley, salt, and pepper.

Arrange paupiettes on serving plates, spoon on butter sauce, and serve immediately.

Turkey Breast with Lemon Butter

Somehow the occasion
always seems special
when turkey is served.
Sliced thinly, turkey
breast offers the elegance
of veal, without the
expense, and with a
great deal more flavor.
If you prefer, instead
of sautéing, the turkey
slices can be cooked
about a minute per side
on a very hot grill.

6 servings

1 (2½-pound) boneless, skinless turkey breast
salt and freshly ground black pepper to taste
2 tablespoons olive oil
7 tablespoons unsalted butter, cold
10 shallots, finely diced
juice of 1½ lemons
½ cup chicken stock or canned broth
½ teaspoon salt
½ teaspoon freshly ground black pepper
½ teaspoon chopped fresh parsley

Carefully trim turkey of any tendons or cartilage and slice across grain into ½-inch slices. Place between 2 layers of plastic wrap and flatten by pressing with flat side of a mallet until ¼-inch thick. Season all over with salt and pepper.

Heat olive oil in a large heavy skillet over high heat. Sauté turkey about 1 minute per side and set aside in a warm place.

Melt 3 tablespoons butter in a medium sauté pan over medium-high heat. Cook shallots until soft, about 2 minutes. Add lemon juice and chicken stock, and bring to a boil. Reduce by half. Break remaining cold butter into small pieces and whisk into pan until smooth. Remove from heat. Stir in salt, pepper, and parsley and reserve.

Arrange escalopes over individual beds of Sautéed Mustard Greens (page 169) or collard greens and spoon over lemon butter sauce. Serve immediately.

Braised Duck with Red Curry

Lime juice and coconut milk give this authentic Thai curry a fruity, almost tropical taste—compared to the earthier Indian curries. This bold stew needs nothing more than a generous bed of rice to balance its flavors.

6 servings

2 (5-pound) ducks
salt and freshly ground black pepper to taste
¼ cup rendered duck fat (page 236) or vegetable oil
16 medium shallots, thinly sliced
8 garlic cloves, minced
2 tablespoons freshly grated ginger (page 235)
¼ cup Thai red curry paste (page 235)
5 cups Brown Duck Stock (page 58) or chicken stock
¼ cup Thai Fish Sauce (page 235)
1 (14-ounce) can coconut milk (page 233)
3 tablespoons palm sugar (page 234) or brown sugar
¼ cup fresh lime juice
2 bunches cilantro, chopped, stems trimmed
2 limes, peeled and diced
1 bunch scallions, the white and ½ the green part, trimmed, and
    thinly sliced along diagonal

Bone ducks and remove the skin. (You can ask a butcher to do this, reserving the carcass for stock making and skin for rendering.) Cut breasts in half, then into about 3 pieces across the width. Chop legs and thighs into about 4 pieces each. (Remember: You want to start with generous pieces of meat, since they will shrink when cooked. Don't worry about cleaning the tendons, since they will soften with long cooking.) Sprinkle meat with salt and pepper.

Heat rendered fat in a large, heavy-bottomed Dutch oven over high heat. Brown duck on all sides, then transfer meat to a platter. Reduce heat to medium-low and cook shallots until brown. Add garlic and ginger, cook about a minute, then add curry paste. Cook, stirring constantly, about 3 minutes. Return duck meat to pot along with Brown Duck Stock and cook at a simmer, uncovered, until meat is tender, about 40 minutes.

(*continued*)

With a slotted spoon, transfer meat to a platter and reserve in a warm place. Puree sauce in a blender and strain back into pot. Cook over high heat until liquid is reduced by one third. Stir in Thai Fish Sauce, coconut milk, sugar, and lime juice, and remove from heat. Stir duck back into warm sauce. Ladle stew over Basmati Rice (page 146). Garnish with remaining ingredients and serve immediately.

Warm Confit of Duck with Madeira Sauce

1 recipe Confit of Duck (page 103)
8 shallots, finely minced
1 cup Madeira
2 cups Brown Duck Stock (page 58) or Brown Veal Stock (page 57)
6 tablespoons unsalted butter, cold

Preheat oven to 350°F. Arrange skinless pieces of duck in a roasting pan, cover with aluminum foil, and bake 30 minutes to reheat.

Meanwhile, cook shallots and Madeira in a medium saucepan over high heat until wine is reduced by half. Add stock and reduce again by half. Break butter into small pieces and whisk into sauce until completely smooth. Top with Madeira Sauce.

Try this in place of roasted duck at a holiday dinner. It's much less greasy and, best of all, the duck can be made weeks in advance! We like to serve warm duck on top of Roasted Potatoes (page 145).

6 servings

Confit of Duck

Don't let the quantity of fat in this recipe alarm you. While the duck is slowly cooking, its interior fat melts, leaving the silky, smooth meat without a trace of grease. This technique, originally used for preserving, must be started at least a day in advance. The cooked duck can then be held as long as 4 weeks without any loss of quality.

6 servings

2 (5-pound) ducks
2 teaspoons salt
2 tablespoons black peppercorns, cracked (page 235)
6 cups rendered duck or pork fat (page 236)
6 garlic cloves, peeled

Remove ducks' legs and breasts, saving remaining bones and wings for Brown Duck Stock (page 58). Leaving bones and skin attached, chop breasts into halves. Remove tips of drumsticks to use in stock.

Sprinkle all over with salt and pepper, and set aside at room temperature 45 minutes. Then place duck pieces in a Dutch oven with rendered fat and garlic. Cook over low heat, uncovered, 1½ to 2 hours. To test for doneness, pierce with a sharp fork. It should fall off fork when shaken.

Transfer duck pieces to a medium baking dish and add the fat. Let cool to room temperature, cover with plastic wrap, and refrigerate at least 24 hours or as long as 4 weeks. Before serving, lift duck pieces out of fat. Remove and discard skin and any excess fat. Serve duck hot or cold.

Fish and Shellfish

It goes against our grain to give recipes for fish in the same style as we have for meat and poultry, since the key to fish cookery is its flexibility. Unlike a cut of meat that must be cooked a certain way, then served with a particular sauce, fish's mild flavor invites experimentation. So while we might specify swordfish, for example, with the mustard and chopped shallots, you could easily substitute salmon or tuna.

The best fish for grilling are the oily ones like tuna, swordfish, salmon, sturgeon, mackerel, or mahi mahi to name a few. Any of the cool, uncooked sauces—such as the one on page 128—served with grilled fillets make lovely, quick dinners.

For roasting or poaching, such as Cold Poached Salmon with Tomato and Herbs (page 127), use the flakier fish that tend to fall apart on the grill: red snapper, black cod, sea bass, salmon, whitefish, turbot, orange roughy, halibut, and monkfish. We dress them up with assorted mild vegetable-based cream sauces, called coulis, for more formal presentations. Once again, feel free to mix and match the sauces according to taste and what is available at your fish market. The best fish cookery is always the simplest.

Roasted Black Cod with Coulis of Horseradish

Horseradish and lime make this a thin coulis that's a bit acidic—a good match for light, buttery black cod.

6 servings

COULIS OF HORSERADISH

5 tablespoons unsalted butter, cold

4 shallots, thinly sliced

4 mushrooms, thinly sliced

1 teaspoon salt

¼ teaspoon freshly ground black pepper

1½ cups dry white wine

1½ cups clam juice or Fish Stock (page 56)

1½ cups heavy cream

juice of 1 lime

4 dashes of Tabasco

6 tablespoons freshly grated horseradish

6 (7-ounce) black cod fillets

salt and freshly ground black pepper to taste

4 tablespoons (½ stick) unsalted butter

3 limes, thinly sliced, daikon spiced sprouts (page 233), and freshly grated horseradish for garnish

Melt 2 tablespoons butter in a medium saucepan over low heat. Add shallots, mushrooms, salt, and pepper, and cook until soft. Turn heat to high, add wine, and reduce by half. Add clam juice or stock and reduce again by half. Strain through a medium sieve back into pan.

Preheat oven to 450°F.

Return pan to high heat, add cream, and reduce by half, being careful not to overreduce. (If the sauce should break at this point, you can bring it back together with a quick turn in the blender.) Stir in lime juice, Tabasco, and horseradish. Break remaining 3 tablespoons cold butter into small pieces and whisk into sauce until smooth. Reserve in a warm place.

Season fillets all over with salt and pepper. Melt remaining 4 tablespoons butter in a large skillet over high heat. Sauté fish for 1 minute. Turn over, transfer to oven, and bake, uncovered, for 3 to 5 minutes.

Arrange fish on individual plates. Spoon on warm sauce and garnish with slices of lime, daikon spiced sprouts, and more fresh horseradish. Serve immediately.

Grilled Swordfish with Mustard

Our secret formula for last-minute summer entertaining—this entire dish can be put together in about 10 minutes. Use the freshest shallots and chives, however, so that each flavor is cool, clear, and refreshing.

6 servings

5 tablespoons Dijon mustard
2 tablespoons olive oil
6 tablespoons clam juice
½ cup minced shallots
½ cup chopped fresh chives
½ teaspoon freshly ground black pepper
6 (7-ounce) swordfish fillets
salt and freshly ground black pepper to taste
olive oil for brushing

Preheat grill as hot as possible.

Mix mustard, olive oil, clam juice, shallots, chives, and pepper in a small bowl. Cover with plastic wrap and reserve.

Season fish all over with salt and pepper. Grill about 3 minutes per side, brushing with olive oil after turning. Transfer onto serving plates, spoon sauce, place grilled fish on sauce, and serve immediately. Goes nicely with Sautéed Mustard Greens (page 169).

Roasted Sea Bass with White Port and Roasted Pepper Sauce

The sweetness of port wine is balanced by the smoky roasted peppers and salty olives in this versatile warm fish sauce. It goes equally well with roasted red snapper or halibut.

6 servings

WHITE PORT AND ROASTED PEPPER SAUCE

2 tablespoons unsalted butter

6 mushrooms, thinly sliced

6 shallots, thinly sliced

salt and freshly ground black pepper to taste

2 cups white port wine

2 cups clam juice or Fish Stock (page 56)

2 cups heavy cream

2 red bell peppers, roasted, peeled, seeded, and julienned (page 236)

2 cups kalamata olives, sliced off pit and julienned

6 (7-ounce) sea bass fillets

salt and freshly ground black pepper to taste

4 tablespoons (½ stick) unsalted butter

1 bunch chives, chopped, for garnish

Melt butter in a medium saucepan over low heat. Add mushrooms, shallots, salt, and pepper, and cook until soft, about 10 minutes.

Preheat oven to 450°F.

Raise heat to high, add port, and reduce by half. Add clam juice or Fish Stock and reduce again by half. Add cream and reduce one more time by half. Remove from the heat, strain sauce, and stir in peppers and olives. Reserve in a warm place.

Season fillets all over with salt and pepper. Melt remaining 4 tablespoons butter in a large skillet over high heat. Sauté fish for 1 minute. Turn over, transfer to oven, and bake, uncovered, for 3 to 5 minutes.

Arrange fish on individual plates. Spoon on warm sauce and garnish with chopped chives. Serve immediately.

Grilled Whole Salmon

In this dramatic outdoor presentation, the entire fish is first wrapped in greens, then seared on a red-hot grill. The greens protect the fish and impart a delicate, tart flavor before they blacken and remain on the grill. Make sure your grill is extremely hot and well seasoned before proceeding. Ideal for a summer buffet.

8 to 10 servings

MARINADE

½ cup cracked black pepper (page 235)

2 cups san bai su (page 234)

½ cup fresh lemon juice

¾ cup sesame oil

6 tablespoons sesame tahini (page 235)

1 (7-pound) salmon, cleaned, with head and tail on

2 bunches collard greens, washed, untrimmed

Japanese wasabi powder and white vinegar for garnish (optional)

Combine marinade ingredients in a glass or ceramic roasting pan. Whisk to combine. Using a sharp knife, score several diagonal lines along the length of fish, down to spine, on either side. Marinate 2 to 4 hours at room temperature.

After marination, preheat grill or broiler.

Blanch greens in a large pot of boiling, salted water, just until the water returns to a boil. Refresh with iced water and drain.

On a large baking sheet, arrange greens, overlapping, to form a rectangle as long as the fish and more than twice as wide. Place fish in middle and wrap with greens so only the head and tail are exposed. The dampness will make them cling.

Transfer fish to grill, reserving marinade. Cook 7 to 12 minutes per side, until greens, head, and tail blacken. It will take 2 spatulas, one at the head and one at the tail, to turn fish. Don't be concerned about greens sticking.

To test for doneness, try to pull out a dorsal fin from top of fish. If it slides out easily fish is done.

To serve, place whole fish on a serving platter. Using a dull knife and soup spoon, scrape off any remaining skin and remove fins.

Spoon half reserved marinade over top. Cut along spine first and serve the top fillet. Lift tail, insert knife between bones and flesh, and run it along length. All (or most) bones should easily lift out. Spoon on remaining marinade and serve second fillet.

As an optional garnish, mix dry Japanese wasabi powder with a few drops of vinegar to form a paste. Serve small squares alongside fish or in ramekins with the marinade for dipping.

Grilled Tuna with Chopped Tomatoes and Spinach Pesto

We like to emphasize the simplicity of grilled fish by serving it with fresh, uncomplicated accompaniments like Chopped Tomatoes and Spinach Pesto. With its red and green stripes, this easy dish is a good-looking entrée.

6 servings

Chopped Tomatoes

8 tomatoes, peeled, seeded, and diced (page 236)
½ cup olive oil
1½ teaspoons salt
¼ teaspoon freshly ground black pepper

Mix all ingredients in a bowl and reserve in the refrigerator.
makes 4 cups

Spinach Pesto

3 tablespoons olive oil
2 bunches spinach, stems trimmed, washed, and dried
½ teaspoon salt
¼ teaspoon freshly ground black pepper
2 tablespoons pureed garlic (page 236)

Heat oil in a large skillet over high heat. Add spinach, salt, and pepper and cook briefly until spinach begins to wilt. Add garlic and cook, stirring constantly, until aroma is released. Puree in a food processor or blender, along with the liquid in pan, until smooth. Chill until serving time.

makes 1 cup

6 (7-ounce) tuna fillets
salt and freshly ground black pepper to taste

Preheat grill as hot as possible. Season fish all over with salt and pepper, and grill 3 to 6 minutes per side. The centers should remain bright pink.

Coat serving plates with Chopped Tomatoes. Using a squirt bottle or a spoon, arrange Spinach Pesto in generous stripes over tomatoes. Top with grilled fish and serve immediately.

Roasted Monkfish with Coulis of Turnips

Monkfish, also known as lotte or angler, has an exceptionally strong flavor and meaty texture that goes well with earthy turnips. Because turnips are so absorbent, keep your eye on this sauce. It will reduce quickly.

6 servings

COULIS OF TURNIPS

10 tablespoons (1 stick plus 2 tablespoons) unsalted butter, cold
6 mushrooms, thinly sliced
1 leek, white and light green parts, cut in half lengthwise and thinly sliced
6 shallots, thinly sliced
½ teaspoon salt
¼ teaspoon freshly ground black pepper
3 turnips, peeled, cut in half, and thinly sliced
1 cup dry white wine
4 cups clam juice or Fish Stock (page 56)
1½ cups heavy cream
juice of ½ lemon
2 tablespoons Tabasco

6 (7-ounce) monkfish fillets
salt and freshly ground black pepper to taste
4 tablespoons (½ stick) unsalted butter
1½ ounces hard smoked beef sausage, julienned (optional garnish)

Melt 2 tablespoons butter in a medium saucepan over low heat. Add mushrooms, leek, shallots, salt, and pepper, and cook until soft but not colored, about 10 minutes. Add turnips and continue cooking over low heat, stirring occasionally, until they begin to soften, about 5 minutes.

(continued)

Add wine, turn heat to high, and reduce by half. Add clam juice and reduce again by half. Add cream, bring to a boil, and remove from heat.

Preheat oven to 450°F. Puree cream mixture in a blender until smooth. Pass through a medium strainer back into pan. Bring back to a boil. Break remaining cold butter into small pieces and whisk into sauce until smooth. (You can thin the sauce with additional clam juice or stock, if necessary.) Stir in lemon juice and Tabasco, and reserve.

Season fillets all over with salt and pepper. Melt remaining 4 tablespoons butter in a large skillet over high heat. Sauté fish 1 minute. Turn over, transfer to the oven, and bake, uncovered, for 3 to 5 minutes.

Slice fillets and arrange on individual plates. Spoon on warm sauce and serve immediately. For optional garnish, sauté sausage strips in a dry pan until warmed through and sprinkle over top.

Sauteed Shrimps with Tomatoes and Pernod

*It takes a strong
shellfish like shrimp or
sea scallops to stand up
to the distinctive anise-
flavored, French aperitif
Pernod. Serve this
soupy dish over a bed of
fettuccine with plenty of
crusty French bread to
sop up the delicious
sauce.*

4 servings

6 large tomatoes, peeled, seeded, and diced (page 236)
2 tablespoons Pernod
2 teaspoons salt
½ teaspoon freshly ground black pepper
2½ pounds medium shrimp, peeled and deveined
salt and freshly ground black pepper to taste
8 tablespoons (1 stick) unsalted butter, cold
¼ pound Chinese snow peas, julienned
1 bunch chervil, stems trimmed, chopped, for garnish

Puree tomatoes in a blender until smooth. If dry, add a tablespoon or 2 of water. Pass through a medium strainer into a mixing bowl.
Stir in Pernod, salt, and pepper. Reserve.

Season shrimps with salt and pepper. Melt 4 tablespoons butter
in a large skillet over high heat. Sauté shrimps until pink-orange, about
1 minute per side. With a slotted spoon, transfer shrimp to a platter,
leaving butter in pan.

Add reserved tomato sauce and julienned snow peas. Bring to
a boil and cook until reduced by about one-third. Adjust seasonings to
taste.

Break remaining butter in small pieces and stir into sauce
along with shrimp. Once smooth, remove from heat, and ladle over
bowls of warm fettuccine. Garnish with chervil and serve immediately.

Roasted Halibut with Coulis of Leeks

Our vegetable coulis are rich and creamy sauces. Choose a light, flavorful starter like Thai Melon Salad (page 8) or Chinese Sausage Salad (page 9) if you are planning to serve this type of entrée at a dinner party.

6 servings

COULIS OF LEEKS

2 leeks
10 tablespoons (1 stick plus 2 tablespoons)
   unsalted butter, cold
6 shallots, sliced
6 mushrooms, thinly sliced
1 teaspoon salt
¼ teaspoon freshly ground black pepper
1 cup dry white wine
2 cups clam juice or Fish Stock (page 56)
1 cup heavy cream
3 dashes of Tabasco
1 teaspoon fresh lemon juice

6 (7-ounce) halibut fillets
salt and freshly ground black pepper to taste
4 tablespoons (½ stick) unsalted butter

Trim and discard dark green part of leeks and slice whites in half lengthwise. Wash in cold, running water and cut across width in ¼-inch slices.

Melt 2 tablespoons butter in a medium saucepan over low heat. Add leeks, shallots, mushrooms, salt, and pepper. Cook until soft but not colored, about 10 minutes. Add wine, turn heat to high, and reduce by half. Add clam juice and reduce again by half. Add cream, bring to a boil, and remove from heat.

Preheat the oven to 450°F.

Puree cream mixture in a blender until smooth, then strain. Return to pan and bring back to a boil. Break remaining cold butter into small pieces and whisk into sauce until smooth. Stir in Tabasco and lemon juice. Set aside in a warm place.

Season fillets all over with salt and pepper. Melt remaining 4 tablespoons butter in a large skillet over high heat. Sauté fish 1 minute. Turn over, transfer to oven, and bake, uncovered, for 3 to 5 minutes.

Arrange fish on serving plates. Top with sauce and serve immediately.

Variation: To add a touch of color and crunch, try deep-frying a leek as garnish for this white dish. Cut leek in thirds lengthwise, then finely julienne. Deep-fry in 2 cups vegetable oil, until golden, about 1½ minutes. Drain on paper towels, and serve alongside the fish.

Portuguese Mussel and Cockle Stew

This dish is a great crowd pleaser. All the ingredients can be measured and chopped in advance. At the last minute, just add the liquids and boil for about 10 minutes for a great homemade fish stew.

6 servings

2 pounds mussels

2 pounds cockles (littleneck or other small clams may be substituted)

1 red bell pepper

1 green bell pepper

1 yellow bell pepper

1 medium yellow Spanish onion

1 small zucchini, with skin

1 small yellow crookneck squash, with skin

1 hard, smoked linguica sausage (about 6 ounces) or prosciutto

1 large ripe tomato, peeled, seeded, and diced (page 235)

½ cup kalamata olives, cut from the pit and julienned

2 to 3 cups well-seasoned Fish Stock (page 56) or clam juice

¾ cup white port wine

freshly ground black pepper to taste

2 tablespoons chopped fresh parsley for garnish

Wash mussels and cockles or clams under cold running water and scrub with a stiff brush. Remove mussels' beards by sharply pulling. Place shellfish in a large bowl, cover with a wet towel, and reserve in refrigerator.

Core and seed bell peppers. Cut into fine julienne, about 2 inches long. Cut onion, zucchini, and yellow squash into similar julienne. Cut sausage or prosciutto into thin 2-inch lengths and finely julienne.

Combine shellfish, julienned vegetables, sausage, tomato, olives, Fish Stock, port, and pepper in a large stockpot or Dutch oven. Cover and cook over high heat until shells open, about 8 to 10 minutes. Taste before adjusting seasonings since shellfish and bottled clam juice are quite salty. Ladle into soup bowls, sprinkle with chopped parsley, and serve immediately.

Crayfish Casserole

This hot and spicy Cajun casserole can be combined in advance and baked right before serving. Serve with a green salad at an informal winter gathering.

6 servings

5 tablespoons olive oil

2 medium onions, diced

1 tablespoon pureed garlic (page 235)

1 teaspoon salt

1 teaspoon paprika

1 teaspoon ground cumin

½ teaspoon cayenne pepper

½ teaspoon freshly grated nutmeg

½ teaspoon cinnamon

¼ teaspoon ground cloves

6 ounces smoked sausage or salami, julienned

2 bell peppers, red and green, julienned

2 tomatoes, peeled, seeded, and diced (page 236)

2 cups bottled clam juice

1 cup tomato juice

5 cups cooked rice

1½ pounds cleaned, cooked crayfish tails or medium shrimp

1½ cups fine dry bread crumbs

Preheat oven to 350°F.

Heat 3 tablespoons oil in a large skillet over medium-high heat. Sauté onions until golden. Add all spices and cook just until aromas are released, 1 to 2 minutes.

Reduce heat to moderate. Add smoked sausage or salami, bell peppers, tomatoes, clam juice, tomato juice, rice, and crayfish or shrimp. Stir to combine. Transfer to a 10-cup ovenproof casserole or 6 individual casseroles.

Mix bread crumbs with remaining 2 tablespoons of oil to form a paste. Sprinkle evenly over top. Bake until bubbly, about 20 minutes. Serve immediately.

Vegetarian Entrées

Here is a small sample of the vegetable dishes that we serve as entrées. They are all satisfying and special enough to serve to guests—and not necessarily vegetarians! ✕

Eggplant Spinach Curry

For a complete vegetarian meal, serve this light, flavorful stew over a bed of Basmati Rice (page 146) a dal, and a raita (page 182–183) and spicy Pickled Tomatoes (page 188).

4 entrées or 6 accompaniments

1 large eggplant, diced, with skin
2 teaspoons coarse salt for sprinkling
2 tablespoons black mustard seeds (page 232)
6 tablespoons clarified butter (page 235)
1 large onion, diced
½ teaspoon salt
2 tablespoons pureed garlic (page 236)
2 tablespoons freshly grated ginger (page 235)
1 teaspoon ground cumin
½ teaspoon ground coriander
½ teaspoon ground cardamom
½ teaspoon garam masala (page 233)
¼ teaspoon turmeric
¼ teaspoon ground cloves
¼ teaspoon cayenne pepper
2 tomatoes, peeled, seeded, and diced (page 236)
1 cup water
1 tablespoon palm sugar (page 234) or brown sugar
2 bunches spinach, stems removed, washed, and cut in 2-inch pieces

Place eggplant in a colander, sprinkle with coarse salt, and let stand for 30 minutes to sweat. Pat dry with paper towels.

Place mustard seeds in a small, dry sauté pan and cook over moderate heat until they turn gray and start popping. Remove from heat and reserve.

Heat ¼ cup clarified butter in a large skillet over moderate heat. Sauté eggplant, stirring occasionally, until soft and golden. Remove from heat and reserve in a bowl with mustard seeds.

Heat remaining butter in a medium saucepan over medium-high heat. Add onions and salt. Sauté until onions are golden and soft. Add garlic and ginger, cook just until aromas are released, then stir in all spices. Cook an additional minute, stirring constantly, to blend spices and prevent scorching.

Add tomatoes, water, and sugar. Turn heat to high and bring to a boil. Add spinach, bring back to a boil, and stir in eggplant mixture. When eggplant is heated through, about 2 minutes, remove from heat and serve.

Chanterelle Risotto

Woodsy chanterelle mushrooms underline the heartiness of risotto, the delicious short-grained Italian rice dish. Serve with a bitter green salad, such as watercress, for a satisfying supper.

4 to 6 servings

1½ pounds chanterelle mushrooms
¼ cup olive oil
4 tablespoons (½ stick) unsalted butter
2 large onions, diced
1 teaspoon salt
1 teaspoon freshly ground black pepper
1 tablespoon pureed garlic (page 236)
½ cup brandy
1 pound arborio rice (available in Italian specialty shops)
2 bay leaves
9 cups chicken stock or canned broth, warm
1 cup Parmesan cheese

Wipe mushrooms clean with a damp paper towel. Break into bite-sized pieces and reserve.

Heat oil and butter in a large saucepan over medium-low heat. Cook onions with salt and pepper until soft and translucent. Stir in garlic and cook until aroma is released. Add mushrooms and sauté until golden. Add brandy, turn heat to high, and scrape bottom of pan with a wooden spoon to release brown bits.

Light alcohol with a match. When flame subsides, add rice and sauté until slightly colored. Add bay leaves and 1½ cups chicken stock. Bring to a boil, reduce heat to medium, and cook until nearly dry.

Once the liquid is evaporated, briefly sauté rice. Then, add stock 1½ cups at a time, constantly stirring with a wooden spoon until absorbed. Repeat procedure, stirring constantly and briefly sautéing between additions, until all stock has been absorbed. You must *constantly* stir while cooking rice. When done, the rice should be glazed outside and soft throughout. It takes approximately 20 minutes to add all the stock. Stir in Parmesan cheese. Serve immediately.

Potato Pea Curry

In India, where cooks work with a limited number of native ingredients, spices are considered as important as the main ingredient. We urge you to keep on hand the dry spices listed here, in place of curry powder, to create your own curries. Remember, authentic curries are not necessarily hot—always adjust the seasonings to suit your taste.

4 entrées or 6
accompaniments

3 large baking potatoes, peeled
½ cup clarified butter (page 235)
2 large onions, diced
1 tablespoon pureed garlic (page 236)
1 tablespoon freshly grated ginger (page 235)
2½ tablespoons ground cumin
1 teaspoon turmeric
½ tablespoon ground coriander
½ tablespoon dried red pepper flakes
3 tomatoes, peeled, seeded, and diced (page 236)
3 cups chicken stock or water
1 tablespoon salt
2 cups fresh or frozen peas, thawed
1 tablespoon palm sugar (page 234) or brown sugar
¼ cup fresh lime juice
1 bunch fresh cilantro, roughly chopped

Cut potatoes into ½-inch dice. Place in a bowl and rinse with cold running water until water runs clear, to remove excess starch.

Heat ¼ cup clarified butter in a medium saucepan over medium-high heat. Sauté onions until brown. At same time, heat remaining clarified butter in a large skillet over moderate heat. Fry potatoes until golden and add sautéed onions.

Add garlic and ginger, and cook just long enough to release their aromas. Remove from heat and add cumin, turmeric, coriander, and pepper flakes. Return pan to moderate heat. Stir in tomatoes, chicken stock or water, and salt.

Simmer, uncovered, until potatoes are soft, about 15 minutes. Add remaining ingredients and cook until peas are heated through. Adjust seasonings and serve immediately.

Vegetable Vermicelli

Inspired by partner Sue, this colorful one-dish meal is a favorite, an abundant array of fresh vegetables julienne-cut to match the shape of the pasta. Although the ingredient list is long, it is an easy dish to prepare—one that meat eaters will love as much as vegetarians.

6 servings

1 pound white or ½ pound oyster or wild mushrooms
1 large leek, white and light green parts, washed
1 large turnip, peeled
1 large carrot, peeled
1 zucchini, with skin
1 yellow crookneck squash, with skin
¼ pound Chinese snow peas
5 tablespoons unsalted butter, cold
1½ tablespoons pureed garlic (page 236)
1 teaspoon cracked pepper (page 235)
1½ tablespoons salt
1 large tomato, peeled, seeded, and diced (page 236)
1½ cups tomato juice
1 tablespoon fresh lemon juice
1 cup water
2 cups freshly grated Parmesan cheese
1½ pounds vermicelli
grated Parmesan cheese and chopped chives for garnish

Clean vegetables and julienne, ¹⁄₁₆ inch by 3 inches.

Melt 3 tablespoons butter in a large skillet over medium-high heat. Cook mushrooms until slightly colored. Add garlic, cook briefly, and reduce heat to moderate. Add leeks with cracked pepper and cook about a minute. Then add salt, turnip, carrot, zucchini, yellow squash, and snow peas. Cook until vegetables soften, about 3 minutes.

Add tomatoes, tomato juice, lemon juice, and water. Bring to a boil and whisk in remaining 2 tablespoons butter. Remove from heat and stir in Parmesan cheese.

Bring a stockpot of salted water to a boil. Cook vermicelli al dente, timed so that pasta is done just when vegetables are cooked. Drain, transfer to vegetable mixture, toss to combine. Ladle into bowls, garnish with grated Parmesan and chives. Serve immediately.

Main Course Salads

Most of these recipes grew out of our feeling that more and more people are craving lighter, fresher, and healthier meals. In other words, people are eating their vegetables. This selection best captures the way we feel people are eating now.

Smoked Chicken Salad

If you have a good-sized grill, you can easily smoke chicken or turkey outside. Build your fire on one side of the grill and place an oven thermometer on the grate on the other side. When it registers 350°F, place the chicken on the side opposite the fire, cover, and cook about 1½ hours. At the halfway point, you can toss a handful of water-soaked hickory chips on the coals for extra flavor. Or, use our fail-safe stovetop method here.

4 to 6 servings

1 cup hickory chips, soaked in water 1 hour
3 chicken legs, with thighs
salt and freshly ground black pepper to taste
2 small Granny Smith apples, peeled and cored
2 celery stalks, peeled
3 scallions, white and light green parts
½ cup homemade Mayonnaise (page 179)
1 tablespoon red wine vinegar
½ head green leaf lettuce, 1 basket cherry tomatoes, 2 avocados, sliced, 1½ cups Sweet and Sour Red Cabbage (page 173) for garnish

After soaking hickory chips, make a stovetop smoker with that big old pot you've been meaning to throw away. (Or line a good pot with aluminum foil to keep it from aging quickly.) Place chips on bottom of pot and a rack above them.

Season chicken with salt and pepper. Place legs on rack, cover pot, and place on a burner over high heat. When chips start to smoke, reduce heat to moderate and cook chicken about ½ hour per side. The juices should run clear when pierced with a knife. Chill a minimum of 2 hours or as long as a day. When meat is chilled, remove skin and bone, and cut into ½-inch dice for the salad.

Cut apples and celery into ½-inch dice and thinly slice scallions across the width. Combine diced chicken, apples, and scallions with celery, mayonnaise, and vinegar in a large bowl and toss well. Adjust salt and pepper to taste.

Line each serving plate with a bed of lettuce. Divide chicken salad and place a mound in center of each plate. Garnish with cherry tomatoes, avocado slices, Sweet and Sour Red Cabbage, and any other crudités you may have in the refrigerator.

Squid or Octopus Salad

Since people tend to feel strongly about eating squid, we like to place an exotic, spicy salad like this one on a buffet, where people can politely take it or leave it. Another good idea is to serve this refreshing salad as an appetizer before a rich, creamy entrée.

6 servings

1 pound squid or cooked octopus, cleaned and thinly sliced
½ teaspoon salt
½ teaspoon freshly ground black pepper
½ cup Thai Fish Sauce (page 235)
1 cup fresh lime juice
½ cup white vinegar
½ cup clam juice
1 medium red onion, finely diced
3 serrano chiles, finely minced with seeds
2 large tomatoes, peeled, seeded, and diced (page 236)
2 pickling cucumbers or Kirbies, diced with skins (page 234)
1 bunch fresh cilantro, chopped
Tabasco, salt, and pepper to taste

Sprinkle squid with salt and pepper. Blanch until water just returns to a boil. Drain and chill. (Octopus need not be blanched.)

Combine the fish sauce, lime juice, vinegar, clam juice, onion, serrano chiles, tomatoes, cucumbers, and cilantro, and toss well with chilled squid or octopus. Season to taste with Tabasco, salt, and pepper. Serve chilled over a bed of greens.

Scotch Eggs

In this old favorite, hard-cooked eggs are coated with sausage, then dipped in bread crumbs and deep-fried. Feel free to substitute store-bought breakfast sausage for the pork and sage mixture. Serve this hearty dish at an Easter brunch with homemade muffins and champagne.

4 servings

1 pound ground pork

3 tablespoons fennel seeds

½ bunch fresh sage, chopped

2 teaspoons salt

1 teaspoon freshly ground black pepper

8 hard-cooked eggs, peeled and chilled

3 cups fine dry bread crumbs

4 eggs, beaten

4 cups vegetable oil

1 recipe Watercress Salad (page 165) made without avocados

2 tomatoes, sliced

Horseradish and Mustard and Mayonnaise (page 178)

Mix together pork, fennel seed, sage, salt, and pepper. Divide into 8 equal portions. Form a patty in your hand with the first portion. Flatten patty, place egg inside, and keep rolling egg and meat in the palms of your hands, until a thin layer of meat coats the egg. Repeat this procedure until all eggs are coated with pork mixture. Chill 20 minutes.

Dip chilled, coated eggs first in bread crumbs, then in eggs and bread crumbs again. Chill 15 minutes. Dip again in eggs, then bread crumbs, and reserve in refrigerator.

Preheat oven to 375°F.

Heat oil in a large stockpot or saucepan to deep-fry temperature (350°F). Fry eggs, 2 or 3 at a time, until golden brown, 3 to 5 minutes. Drain on paper towels. Transfer to a roasting pan and bake 10 minutes.

To serve, arrange a bed Watercress Salad on each serving plate. Slice eggs in half and place 4 halves on top of each salad. Garnish with tomato slices and dollops of Horseradish and Mustard and Mayonnaise for dipping. Serve while eggs are warm.

Cold Poached Salmon with Tomato and Herbs

One of several versatile uncooked sauces that we serve with fish is Tomato and Herbs. This one can be served with grilled tuna as well as poached salmon. And the oil can be omitted for even fewer calories. In the summertime this elegant entrée can be taken on picnics with other good travelers like Roasted Red Peppers with Feta (page 22) and Parsnip Chips (page 157).

6 servings

6 (6-ounce) skinless salmon fillets
salt and freshly ground black pepper to taste
3 cups Fish Stock (page 56) or clam juice

TOMATO AND HERBS

1 bunch oregano
1 bunch basil
1 bunch parsley
1 bunch thyme
6 tomatoes, peeled, seeded, and diced (page 236)
½ cup extra virgin olive oil
1½ teaspoons salt
¼ teaspoon freshly ground black pepper

To poach salmon, preheat oven to 350°F.

Season salmon all over with salt and pepper. Bring stock or juice to a boil in a large ovenproof skillet. Add fish, so they are barely touching, and bring liquid back to a boil. Turn fish over, then cover with a piece of parchment paper coated with olive oil. Transfer to oven and bake 5 minutes. Turn fish over, cover again, bake an additional 2 minutes. (Drain and reserve liquid in the pan for use as stock.) Transfer fish to a platter, cover with plastic wrap, chill until serving time.

For dressing, remove stems and finely chop all herbs. If these fresh herbs are unavailable, substitute chives, mint, marjoram, or chervil. Watercress or the bright yellow leaves inside celery stalks are also preferable to dried herbs. Mix ingredients in a small bowl and refrigerate.

To serve, arrange each fillet on a lettuce-lined serving plate. Spoon on Tomato and Herbs. We like to serve with various garnishes such as radishes, sliced avocado, pickles, or olives around the salmon.

Grilled Tuna with Tomato and Olive Compote

Tuna's strong flavor stands up well to this zesty Spanish-style sauce. If you don't feel like heating the grill to briefly cook the fish, you can sear it in a very hot cast-iron pan instead.

6 servings

TOMATO AND OLIVE COMPOTE

¾ cup olive oil

3 medium onions, julienned

1 teaspoon salt

½ teaspoon freshly ground black pepper

6 tomatoes, peeled, seeded, and diced (page 236)

2 bunches oregano, leaves only, chopped

1 cup small green olives, with pits

3 tablespoons capers, chopped with juice

6 (6-ounce) skinless tuna fillets

salt and freshly ground black pepper to taste

Heat 3 tablespoons oil in a medium skillet over moderate heat. Cook onions with salt until soft, about 10 minutes. Combine remaining ingredients in a bowl. Add cooked onions and chill.

Season tuna all over with salt and pepper. Cook on a very hot, clean grill, about 3 minutes per side. The inside should be bright pink. Transfer to a platter and chill.

To serve, arrange fillets on individual plates. Spoon over Tomato and Olive Compote and serve cold.

Spinach Salad with Yogurt Dressing

Yogurt dressing with garlic and lemon juice—a variation on ranch dressing—accentuates the light, refreshing quality of fresh spinach leaves.

6 servings

2 bunches tender spinach leaves, washed and dried
1 cup white mushroom caps, sliced
Yogurt Dressing, recipe follows
6 slices bacon
3 hard-cooked eggs
2 red bell peppers, roasted, peeled, and seeded (page 236)
1 large ripe tomato, cut in wedges
½ cup crumbled feta cheese

Break spinach into bite-sized pieces and combine in a large bowl with mushrooms. Add enough Yogurt Dressing to coat leaves and toss well. Divide salad among 6 serving plates.

Fry bacon until crisp, drain on paper towels, then break into 1-inch-long strips. Cut eggs in half and slice peppers thinly, lengthwise.

Garnish each salad with bacon strips, bell pepper, tomato wedges, cheese, and half an egg.

Yogurt Dressing

1 tablespoon Dijon mustard
1 tablespoon pureed garlic (page 236)
2 tablespoons fresh lemon juice
1 teaspoon salt
½ teaspoon freshly ground black pepper
½ cup olive oil
1 cup plain yogurt

makes 1½ cups

Mix mustard, garlic, lemon juice, salt, and pepper in a bowl. Gradually whisk in olive oil. Stir in yogurt.

Caesar Salad

Mary Sue's husband Josh's idea of heaven consists of an evening at home with a Caesar Salad, some martinis, a James Bond movie, and Mary Sue. If you want something more, we suggest Tomato and Fennel Soup (page 33) to start.

6 servings

CAESAR SALAD DRESSING

5 anchovies

1 teaspoon cracked black peppercorns (page 235)

½ cup extra virgin olive oil

1 egg

3 tablespoons red wine vinegar

2 tablespoons fresh lemon juice

1 tablespoon pureed garlic (page 236)

2 teaspoons dry mustard

1 teaspoon celery salt

3 dashes of Tabasco

3 dashes of Worcestershire sauce

½ loaf sourdough or hearty French or Italian bread, with crust, diced for croutons

2 medium heads romaine lettuce

½ cup freshly grated Parmesan cheese

Combine anchovies, black pepper, and olive oil in a blender. Puree about 5 minutes until very smooth. Measure and reserve one-third cup for use with croutons.

Bring a small saucepan of water to a boil. Place a refrigerated egg on a slotted spoon and into boiling water. Cook 1½ minutes, remove, and reserve.

Place remaining dressing ingredients in a large bowl and whisk in anchovy mixture. Crack open egg and spoon (including the parts that are uncooked) into mixture. Whisk until well combined. The dressing may be refrigerated at this stage.

Combine reserved anchovy mixture with diced bread in a bowl and toss to coat. Heat a dry cast-iron skillet over medium-high and cook croutons, stirring constantly, until golden and crisp.

Wash and dry lettuce and break into bite-sized pieces. Place in a salad bowl along with dressing and grated Parmesan cheese and toss well. Add toasted croutons, toss again, and serve.

Warm Shredded Chicken Salad

6 boneless, skinless chicken breasts

MARINADE
½ cup sesame oil
2 tablespoons peanut oil
juice of ½ lemon
¼ cup soy sauce
3 tablespoons freshly grated ginger (page 235)
1 tablespoon cornstarch

1 recipe Watercress and Avocado Salad (page 165)
½ cup peanut oil for frying

Expect some smoke and splatter when you make this dish. It's important to heat the pan until it glows, so the marinated chicken gets crisp on the outside and remains tender and juicy inside. The results are delicious!

4 servings

Trim chicken of any excess fat or sinew. Slice, across grain, into 3 × ½-inch strips. Stir marinade ingredients together in a medium bowl. Add chicken strips and toss to coat evenly. Set aside at room temperature, uncovered, 30 minutes. It's important not to marinate any longer, or the acid in the lemon will break down the fibers of the chicken.

Meanwhile arrange Watercress and Avocado Salad on 6 serving plates. Reserve in refrigerator.

To cook chicken, heat a large dry cast-iron skillet over high heat 3 to 5 minutes. Heat peanut oil for frying. Lift chicken strips from marinade, one at a time, and add to pan, standing as far away as possible to avoid splatters. Fry until dark golden brown and crisp, about 1 minute per side. Arrange about 8 hot chicken strips on each salad in a spoke pattern. Serve immediately.

Cold Smoked Black Cod with Potato Salad Vinaigrette

A buttery fish like black cod, salmon, or sturgeon is delicious smoked. Served on a bed of thinly sliced Potato Salad Vinaigrette, this one-dish meal is great for a hot weather lunch.

6 servings

1 cup hickory chips

BRINE

½ cup coarse salt
½ large onion, sliced
3 tablespoons brown sugar
3 bay leaves
1 tablespoon dry mustard
1 1-inch length fresh ginger, sliced thinly
1 teaspoon black peppercorns
¼ teaspoon whole allspice
¼ teaspoon whole cloves
¼ teaspoon freshly grated nutmeg
2 cups water

6 (6-ounce) black cod fillets
1 recipe Potato Salad Vinaigrette (page 152)

Soak hickory chips in water for an hour. Meanwhile, combine brine ingredients in a medium saucepan. Bring to a boil, strain into a ceramic or glass roasting pan, and chill. When cool, marinate fish about 15 minutes at room temperature.

Make a stovetop smoker following the instructions for Smoked Chicken Salad (page 124). When chips start smoking, place fish on rack, cover, and cook over moderate heat 10 minutes. Transfer fish to a platter, cover with plastic wrap, and chill.

To serve, line 6 serving plates with a thin layer Potato Salad Vinaigrette. Cover each with a chilled fish fillet and serve.

5 Accompaniments

These are the small dishes that round out a meal. We serve these vegetable accompaniments with each plate—a puree, a chip, and a sautéed or baked vegetable—to give diners a variety of tastes and textures to try.

These dishes can meet a wide variety of needs. Many can easily be served as starters, salads, or even week-night suppers with perhaps some bread or fruit and cheese. Be creative. Why limit yourself to a meat and vegetable for dinner when you can get your protein just as well from a beautiful Thai Bean Salad (page 138)? Have fun.

Beans

Lentil and Walnut Salad

This inexpensive salad combines the earthiness of lentils and nuts with a refreshing vinaigrette. It can be prepared entirely in advance.

6 servings

2 cups lentils
¼ cup red wine vinegar
¾ cup extra virgin olive oil
½ tablespoon dry mustard
½ teaspoon salt
¼ teaspoon freshly ground black pepper
2 bunches scallions, thinly sliced
2 cups walnuts, roughly chopped

Pick over lentils to remove dirt or pebbles, then rinse in cold, running water until water runs clear. Place lentils in a large pot, add enough water to cover, and bring to a boil. Reduce to a simmer and cook, uncovered, 15 to 20 minutes, until beans are done but not pasty. Drain in a colander.

Whisk red wine vinegar, olive oil, mustard, salt, and pepper together to form a vinaigrette.

While lentils are still warm, combine with scallions and walnuts in a large bowl. Pour on dressing and toss. Chill until serving time.

Chopped Tofu with Parsley

Tofu is great for offsetting strong, spicy foods. The parsley in this recipe adds a fresh flavor to the tofu and garlic. We serve it with our Spicy Cold Soba Noodles (page 143) and Marinated Beef Short Ribs (page 73).

makes 2 cups

1 (14-ounce) package soft tofu
2 tablespoons olive oil
2 tablespoons pureed garlic (page 236)
1 cup finely chopped fresh parsley
¼ cup Mayonnaise (page 179)
2 tablespoons fresh lemon juice
1½ teaspoons salt
½ teaspoon freshly ground black pepper

Drain tofu of water, wrap in a thin kitchen towel or 4 layers of cheesecloth, and squeeze to remove any excess moisture. Roughly chop and reserve.

Heat oil in a small skillet over low heat. Cook garlic 2 to 3 minutes.

In a bowl, combine tofu, sautéed garlic, parsley, Mayonnaise, lemon juice, salt, and pepper. Mash with a fork until fine. Chill and serve in small ramekins or as a dip for crackers or toasts.

Orange Dal with Ginger and Garlic

Orange dal has a lighter, sweeter quality than darker lentils. For a complete protein, vegetarian lunch, try combining the dal with rice, then topping it with a dollop of yogurt and some crisp fried onions.

6 servings

2 cups orange lentil dal (page 233)
2 tablespoons clarified butter (page 235)
2 large onions, finely diced
1 teaspoon salt
1 teaspoon freshly ground black pepper
2 tablespoons pureed garlic (page 236)
2 tablespoons freshly grated ginger (page 235)
2½ cups chicken stock, canned broth, or water

Spread dal on a cookie sheet and pick out any stones or clumps of dirt. Place in a large bowl and wash under cold, running water until water runs clear, about 10 minutes. Drain in a colander.

Heat butter in a medium saucepan over moderate heat. Sauté onions with salt and pepper until golden brown. Add garlic and ginger, and cook 2 to 3 minutes, stirring occasionally. Add dal and chicken stock or water. Bring to a boil, reduce to a simmer, and cook, covered, 20 minutes. Serve immediately. Dal keeps well for 2 to 3 days. Reheat before serving.

Black Bean Salad with Bell Peppers

This healthy salad has lots of visual appeal, with the finely diced, brightly colored peppers against a dark background. It also travels well for picnics or potlucks and keeps in the refrigerator about 2 days.

6 servings

1½ cup dried black beans, washed
3 bell peppers, preferably red, yellow, and green
¾ cup extra virgin olive oil
⅓ cup red wine vinegar
1 teaspoon salt
1 teaspoon freshly ground black pepper
1 large red onion, diced

Place beans in a large pot with a generous quantity of water. Bring to a boil, reduce to a simmer, and cook, uncovered, until tender, about an hour. Check pot occasionally and add water, if necessary, to cover. To test for doneness, taste a small bean as it will be the last to finish cooking. If tender and smooth inside, all beans are done. Continue cooking if the taste is at all powdery. Drain in a colander.

Meanwhile, core and seed peppers and finely dice. In a large bowl, whisk together olive oil, vinegar, salt, and pepper to form a vinaigrette. Toss in diced peppers and onion, and mix well. Add drained beans, toss again, and chill about 2 hours.

Thai Bean Salad

Mary Sue brought this recipe back from Bangkok, where vendors sell individual portions on the street as a between-meal snack. Serve it on a salad buffet with a strong entrée like Grilled Pepper Steak with Tamarind Chutney (page 74), or as a casual main course.

6 to 8 servings

1 pound Chinese long beans, or green or yellow beans, ends trimmed
2 tomatoes, peeled, seeded, and diced (page 236)
1 small zucchini, grated with skin
1 tablespoon pureed garlic (page 236)
¼ cup palm sugar (page 234) or brown sugar
½ cup Thai Fish Sauce (page 235)
½ cup fresh lime juice
3 or more serrano chiles to taste, stems removed and thinly sliced horizontally, with seeds
3 kaffir lime leaves (page 234) chopped, or 1 teaspoon grated lime zest
½ cup dried shrimp (page 233)
1 cup roasted, unsalted peanuts

Blanch beans in a large pot of boiling, salted water until barely tender, about 1 minute. Immediately refresh in a bowl of iced water. If using long beans, tie each bean in a series of knots, 1 inch apart. Then cut between knots, so each piece has a knot in its center. (If this presentation doesn't appeal to you or long beans are not available, skip the knots. The dish tastes fine with beans cut diagonally into ½-inch lengths.) Combine beans with tomatoes and zucchini in a large bowl and reserve.

In another bowl, mix garlic, palm or brown sugar, Thai Fish Sauce, lime juice, serrano chiles, and lime leaves. Roughly chop shrimp and peanuts. Combine with fish sauce mixture.

Pour dressing over reserved vegetables and toss well. Serve immediately.

Cold Garbanzo and Cucumber Salad

Refreshing cucumbers lighten the hearty beans in this simple winter salad.

6 to 8 servings

¾ cup extra virgin olive oil

2 tablespoons red wine vinegar

1½ teaspoon salt

1½ teaspoons freshly ground black pepper

2 cups canned garbanzo beans, drained

5 pickling cucumbers or Kirbies (page 234), peeled and diced

1 medium red onion, diced

2 tomatoes, peeled, seeded, and diced (page 236)

1 bunch fresh basil, chopped

Combine olive oil, vinegar, salt, and pepper in a large bowl and whisk. Add remaining ingredients, toss and chill.

Green Beans with Scallions

The pureed scallions in the dressing give this green salad a forceful bite. The dressing and beans can be prepared in advance, but always combine at the last minute for the best crunch.

6 servings

2 pounds green and yellow beans (if available), cut into 2-inch lengths diagonally

2 bunches scallions, white and part of green, sliced

1 cup sour cream

1 tablespoon fresh lemon juice

½ teaspoon salt

½ teaspoon freshly ground black pepper

½ cup Mayonnaise (page 179)

Blanch beans in rapidly boiling salted water until water reboils. Immediately refresh in iced water until thoroughly chilled and drain.

In a blender, combine scallions, sour cream, and lemon juice. Pulse a few times to combine, then puree until smooth. Add salt, pepper, and Mayonnaise. Blend just to combine.

Toss beans with pureed scallion dressing. Serve immediately.

Noodles

Spaetzle

Here is a handy recipe that takes about 20 minutes from start to finish—great for last-minute emergencies. Serve these comforting little dumplings with any gravy or sauced dish like our Beef Brisket (page 77).

makes 1 pound

2 eggs
2 egg yolks
½ cup heavy cream
1 cup all-purpose flour
½ teaspoon salt
¼ teaspoon freshly ground black pepper
¼ teaspoon freshly grated nutmeg

Mix eggs, egg yolks, and cream together in a bowl. Add remaining ingredients and mix just until moist.

Bring a large saucepan of water to a boil and reduce to a simmer. Hold a large-holed slotted spoon over simmering water and push about ¼ cup dough at a time through the holes to make dumplings. Sometimes a large-holed colander could suffice. Gently simmer until cooked through, 2 to 3 minutes. Remove with a slotted spoon and transfer to a bowl of iced water. Repeat until all dough is cooked. Reheat Spaetzle in a small amount of cream, or butter with water.

Pasta Salad with Black Olives and Feta

Pasta salads were a mainstay at our first restaurant, City Café, out of necessity. The kitchen was so tiny there was no room for an oven. Of the one hundred varieties we created there, this simple, strong salad remains a favorite.

8 servings

1 tablespoon olive oil
2 tablespoons salt
1 pound pasta, small tubes or shells
¾ cup extra virgin olive oil
1 cup crumbled feta cheese
¾ cup kalamata olives
2 medium tomatoes, peeled, seeded, and diced (page 236)
1 large red onion, diced
3 pickling cucumbers or Kirbies (page 234), peeled and diced
2 bunches oregano, leaves only, chopped
3 dashes of Tabasco
salt and freshly ground black pepper to taste

Bring 1 gallon water to a rolling boil in a large stockpot. Add 1 tablespoon olive oil, salt, and pasta, and cook until al dente, about 6 minutes for fresh and 8 minutes for dry. Drain in a colander and immediately transfer to a large bowl of iced water to cool. Drain well, transfer to another bowl, and toss with ¼ cup extra virgin olive oil.

Mix all remaining ingredients in a bowl. Toss with pasta, adjust seasonings, and serve.

Pasta Salad with Roasted Peppers and Onions

Serve a rich, creamy salad like this before a simple entrée like Turkey Breast with Lemon Butter (page 100) or grilled fish. Or serve it as a main course, with the addition of salami.

4 to 6 servings

1 tablespoon olive oil
2 tablespoons salt
1 pound pasta, small tubes or shells
½ cup extra virgin olive oil
6 red and/or yellow bell peppers
3 medium onions, julienned
1½ teaspoons salt
¼ teaspoon freshly ground black pepper
1 tablespoon pureed garlic (page 236)
1 tablespoon paprika
3 large tomatoes, peeled, seeded, and diced, with juice (page 236)
1½ cups sour cream
3 dashes of Tabasco

Bring 1 gallon water to a rolling boil in a large stockpot. Add 1 tablespoon olive oil, salt, and pasta and cook until al dente, about 6 minutes for fresh and 8 minutes for dry. Drain in a colander and immediately transfer to a large bowl of iced water to cool. Drain well, transfer to another bowl, and toss with ¼ cup extra virgin olive oil. Cover with plastic wrap and set aside at room temperature.

Roast peppers under a preheated broiler or directly over a gas flame until completely charred. Transfer to a plastic bag, tightly close, and set aside to steam about 10 minutes. Then, under cold running water, peel and split open to remove core and seeds. Julienne-slice peppers and reserve.

Heat remaining ¼ cup oil in a large skillet over high heat. Add onions, salt, and pepper, and cook until golden brown. Lower heat to moderate, add garlic, and cook 1 minute, then add paprika, and cook 1 minute more. Add red peppers and tomatoes, cook an additional minute, and remove from heat.

Transfer to a medium bowl and combine with sour cream and Tabasco. Pour over reserved pasta, toss well, and serve.

Variation: Add about half a pound Genoa salami, sliced thinly and julienned, to sautéed onions before adding garlic.

Spicy Cold Soba Noodles

Many of our newer recipes have been inspired by our trips to Asia, where people eat less meat. These Japanese buckwheat noodles are a complete protein when served with a Chopped Tofu with Parsley salad (page 135).

If Chinese chili oil is not available, you can make your own by combining ¼ cup of heated peanut oil with 2 tablespoons of dried red pepper flakes. Let sit about 3 minutes to infuse, and strain out the peppers.

6 servings

⅓ cup soy sauce
1 tablespoon molasses
¼ cup sesame oil
¼ cup tahini (page 235)
¼ cup brown sugar
¼ cup Chinese chili oil
3 tablespoons balsamic or red wine vinegar
½ bunch scallions, white and green parts, thinly sliced
salt to taste
½ pound soba or Japanese buckwheat noodles (page 234)

Place soy sauce in a pan over high heat and reduce by half. Turn heat to low, stir in molasses, and warm briefly. Transfer to a mixing bowl. Add sesame oil, tahini, brown sugar, chili oil, vinegar, and scallions, and whisk to combine. Season to taste with salt, if desired.

Bring a large pot of salted water to a rapid boil. Add noodles, bring back to a boil, and cook, stirring occasionally, until they just begin to soften, about 3 minutes. (Soba noodles can overcook very quickly, so stay nearby.)

Have ready a large bowl of iced water. Drain noodles, plunge in iced water, and drain again. Place in a colander and rinse well under cold running water. Combine noodles and sauce, toss well, and chill.

Pasta Salad with Prosciutto and Peas

With its generous quantity of meat and rich Caesar Salad Dressing, this elegant pasta salad could easily be served as a main course. The key when preparing this or any other pasta salad is to mix the pasta with the other ingredients right before serving.

4 to 6 servings

1 tablespoon olive oil
2 tablespoons salt
1 pound pasta, small tubes or shells
¾ cup extra virgin olive oil
2 cups fresh or frozen peas
3 medium red onions, julienned
¾ pound prosciutto, sliced twice as thick as paper and julienned
½ recipe Caesar Salad Dressing (page 130)

Bring 1 gallon water to a rolling boil in a large stockpot. Add 1 tablespoon olive oil, salt, and pasta, and cook until al dente, about 6 minutes for fresh and 8 minutes for dry. Drain in a colander and immediately transfer to a large bowl of iced water to cool. Drain well, transfer to another bowl, and toss with ¼ cup extra virgin olive oil. Cover with plastic wrap and set aside at room temperature.

Cook peas. Immediately rinse with cold water and reserve.

Heat remaining ½ cup oil in a large skillet over high heat. Add onions and cook until golden. Remove from heat. Transfer to a medium bowl and set aside to cool. Stir in peas, prosciutto, and Caesar dressing. Pour over reserved pasta, toss well, and serve.

Starches

Roasted Potatoes

*These potatoes are as
thin and habit-forming
as potato chips. Serve
with grilled steaks or
chops, or Warm Confit
of Duck with Madeira
Sauce (page 102).*

6 servings

3 large baking potatoes, peeled
¾ cup clarified butter (page 235)
½ teaspoon salt
¼ teaspoon freshly ground black pepper

Preheat oven to 450°F. Slice potatoes as thinly as possible across length. (We like to use a mandoline, although a food processor fitted with a 2-millimeter slicing blade will do just fine.) Rinse potatoes by placing in a large bowl, under cold running water, until water runs clear, about 5 minutes. Drain and pat dry with paper towels.

Combine potatoes with butter, salt, and pepper in a medium bowl. Toss to coat.

Arrange potato slices in 2 or 3 layers on a medium jelly roll pan or baking sheet. Bake 30 to 35 minutes, until the edges are golden brown. Tip pan to drain off excess butter, cut into wedges, and serve immediately.

Basmati Rice

In India, where basmati rice is prized above all others, each harvest is given a vintage, so that people can request a specific year.

6 to 8 servings

2 cups basmati rice (page 232)
3 cups water
1 teaspoon salt
2 teaspoons unsalted butter

Place rice in a bowl and rinse under cold, running water, stirring occasionally, until water runs clear. Drain well.

Combine water, salt, and butter in a medium saucepan and bring to a boil. Add rice, return to a boil, and cover. Reduce to a simmer and cook 10 minutes. Remove from heat and let stand, covered, 5 minutes. Serve immediately.

Fenneled Rice

Aromatic fennel and Pernod give rice a fresh, clean taste. This dish is superb with Chicken Breast with Garlic and Parsley (page 94).

4 to 6 servings

1½ cups basmati rice (page 232)

1 to 2 fennel bulbs

2 tablespoons olive oil

1 teaspoon salt

½ teaspoon freshly ground black pepper

½ cup Pernod

2 cups chicken stock or canned broth

1 tomato, peeled, seeded, and diced (page 236)

Place rice in a bowl and rinse under cold, running water until water runs clear. Drain and reserve.

Remove wispy fennel leaves. Chop and reserve for garnish. Cut bulbs in half and slice thinly across width. Finely dice, discarding hard cores.

Heat oil in a medium saucepan over moderate heat. Add chopped fennel bulbs and stalks, salt, and pepper. Cook, uncovered, until soft. Add Pernod, turn heat to high, and light alcohol with a match. Continue to cook over high heat until liquid is reduced by half. Add reserved rice and chicken stock, and bring to a boil. Cover, reduce to a simmer, and cook 5 minutes. Remove from heat and let sit, with cover on, for 5 minutes.

Stir in tomato. Cover and steam an additional 2 minutes. Adjust seasonings, garnish with reserved fennel leaves, and serve warm.

Bulgur Pilaf

Bulgur, or cracked wheat, is available at health food and Middle Eastern markets. It has a wholesome, nutty taste that we love. A great pilaf to serve beneath Grilled Chicken with Roasted Peppers (page 96).

4 to 6 servings

1 cup bulgur wheat (page 233)
1 cup boiling water
4 tablespoons (½ stick) unsalted butter
1 small onion, diced
3 ounces vermicelli, in small pieces
1 cup chicken stock, canned broth, or water
½ teaspoon salt
½ teaspoon freshly ground black pepper

Combine wheat and water in a bowl and set aside until reconstituted, about 10 minutes.

Melt butter in a medium saucepan over medium-high heat. Sauté onion until golden, about 10 minutes. Add vermicelli and sauté until golden. Stir in reconstituted bulgur, chicken stock, salt, and pepper. Reduce to a simmer and cook, covered, about 10 minutes.

Variation: Stir in a diced, roasted red pepper, along with reconstituted bulgur and stock, for some added color.

Rice Salad with Cumin and Squash

This pretty salad showcases cumin—an ingredient that usually appears in combination with hot spices. A great use for leftover rice, you can serve this versatile dish as a starter, a side dish, or on a salad buffet.

6 servings

1 cup olive oil
½ eggplant, with skin, finely diced
1 small yellow crookneck squash, with skin, finely diced
½ zucchini, with skin, finely diced
1 large red onion, diced
2 teaspoons salt
1 tablespoon pureed garlic (page 236)
2 tablespoons ground cumin
1 large tomato, peeled, seeded, and diced (page 236)
1½ cups cooked rice, preferably basmati (page 232)
2 tablespoons tarragon or red wine vinegar

Heat ½ cup oil in a large skillet over moderate heat. Cook eggplant until soft, about 3 minutes. Add yellow squash and zucchini, and cook about 2 minutes more, stirring occasionally. Transfer vegetables to a bowl and reserve.

Add remaining oil to pan and turn heat to high. Sauté onions with salt until golden brown, about 5 minutes. Stir in garlic and cook briefly. Add cumin and cook an additional minute. Reduce heat to low.

Return vegetables to pan. Add tomato, cooked rice, and vinegar. Stir to combine and remove from heat. Serve warm as a vegetable accompaniment or chilled as a salad.

Spinach Pilaf

Here is a quick, easy pilaf that is terrific with grilled fish or sautéed squid.

4 to 6 servings

4 tablespoons (½ stick) unsalted butter
3 bunches spinach, stems trimmed
2 teaspoons salt
1 large onion, diced
1 tablespoon ground cumin
1 teaspoon ground cardamom
1 teaspoon ground coriander
1 teaspoon ground turmeric
2 cups cooked rice, preferably basmati (page 232)
2 tomatoes, peeled, seeded, and diced (page 236)

Melt 2 tablespoons butter in a large sauté pan over medium-high heat. Sauté spinach with salt just until leaves are wilted. Reserve.

Melt remaining butter in a medium saucepan over medium-high heat. Sauté onions until lightly browned. Reduce heat, add ground spices, and stir briefly. Add cooked rice, tomatoes, and reserved spinach. Cook just enough to heat rice through, stirring well to combine. Serve warm.

Greek Potato Salad

We prefer smooth-textured red potatoes for our light, thinly sliced potato salads. Fresh thyme or sage are good substitutes if oregano is unavailable.

6 servings

2 pounds red potatoes, washed, with skins
1 cup virgin olive oil
3 shallots, chopped
1½ bunches oregano, leaves only, chopped
2 teaspoons fresh lemon juice
1 teaspoon salt
¼ teaspoon freshly ground black pepper

Cut potatoes across width into ⅛-inch slices. Place in a large bowl and wash in cold, running water until water runs clear.

Bring a large pot of salted water to a boil. Add potatoes, bring back to a boil, and cook until slices are barely soft, about 3 to 5 minutes. Drain in a colander.

Combine remaining ingredients in a medium bowl. Add warm potato slices and toss to combine. Serve immediately or chill. Potato salad may be kept in a sealed container in refrigerator 2 to 3 days.

Potato Salad Vinaigrette

The potato slices are as thin and crunchy as lettuce leaves in this refreshing presentation. We serve it in smoked fish sandwiches.

6 servings

6 medium red potatoes, with skins, washed
½ medium red onion, thinly sliced
2 tablespoons red wine vinegar
1 tablespoon plus 1 teaspoon Dijon mustard
½ cup virgin olive oil
1 bunch parsley, leaves only, chopped
2 teaspoons pureed garlic (page 236)
1½ teaspoons salt
dash of freshly ground black pepper

Using a mandoline or food processor, fitted with a 2-millimeter slicing blade, slice potatoes across width as thinly as possible. Place in a large bowl and wash in cold, running water until water runs clear.

Bring a large pot of salted water to a boil. Add potatoes, bring back to a boil, and remove from heat. Drain in a colander. In a medium bowl, toss potatoes with red onion and reserve.

Whisk remaining ingredients in a small bowl to form a vinaigrette. Pour over potatoes and onions, and toss to combine. Serve immediately or refrigerate as long as 2 days.

Purees

Roasted Eggplant with San Bai Su

This flavorful puree can be served hot, chilled, or at room temperature. We use it to round out a plate of grilled chicken and rice or with warm pita triangles as an appetizer.

6 servings

3 medium eggplants
6 tablespoons olive oil
3 tablespoons pureed garlic (page 236)
½ cup san bai su (page 234) or ¼ cup soy sauce
1 tablespoon cayenne pepper
1 teaspoon salt (optional)

Preheat broiler. Place eggplants on a large baking sheet close to flame. Roast as you would peppers, until skin is charred all over and flesh is softened, about 40 minutes. Set aside to cool. Peel and roughly chop meat, reserving juice.

Heat oil in a medium skillet over medium-low heat. Add garlic. Cook gently, stirring occasionally, 1 minute. Stir in remaining ingredients and remove from heat. Season to taste with salt and serve.

Sweet Potato Puree with Honey and Lime

This hearty accompaniment is not too sweet—a great idea for Thanksgiving dinner. You can tell that sweet potatoes and yams are done baking when honeylike droplets form on the skin.

6 servings

5 pounds sweet potatoes, unpeeled
4 tablespoons (½ stick) unsalted butter
1 cup sour cream
2 tablespoons fresh lime juice
2 tablespoons honey
½ teaspoon salt
¼ teaspoon freshly ground black pepper

Preheat oven to 400°F. Bake potatoes until soft, about 45 minutes. Set aside to cool. Then peel, roughly chop, and puree in a food processor, being careful not to overprocess.

Place butter and sour cream in a medium saucepan over medium-low heat. Stir in pureed potatoes and remaining ingredients. Adjust seasonings and serve immediately.

Carrot and Rutabaga Puree

In this puree of winter vegetables, the carrots sweeten and lighten the earthy rutabaga.

6 servings

1 large rutabaga
6 large carrots
5 tablespoons unsalted butter
¼ cup water
salt and freshly ground black pepper to taste

Preheat oven to 350°F.

Peel rutabaga and carrots, and cut into ½-inch slices. Combine with remaining ingredients in a medium saucepan. Cover and bake until tender, 15 to 20 minutes. Finely grind vegetables in a food processor or meat grinder. Adjust seasonings and serve hot.

Mashed Potatoes

*Our authentic all-
American recipe for
everyone's favorite
puree—mashed
potatoes. The key to
fluffy, creamy potatoes
is to combine the
ingredients while warm.
For richer potatoes,
increase the butter and
sour cream to taste.*

6 to 8 servings

2½ pounds baking potatoes, peeled and quartered
1½ tablespoons salt
1 cup sour cream
8 tablespoons (1 stick) unsalted butter
salt and freshly ground black pepper to taste
cracked black pepper for garnish

Place potatoes in a bowl and wash under cold, running water until water runs clear. Place in a medium saucepan with salt. Add enough water to generously cover. Bring to a boil, reduce to a simmer, and cook, uncovered, until soft, about 15 minutes. While potatoes are still warm, mash with a fork, in a food mill, or gently in a food processor.

In a medium saucepan, warm sour cream and butter. Fold warm sour cream mixture into potatoes, add salt and pepper to taste, and serve immediately. Garnish with cracked pepper.

Creamed Spinach

*We never grow tired of
this classic spinach
puree.*

6 servings

3 tablespoons unsalted butter
3 bunches spinach, washed and stems removed
1 small onion, diced
1½ cups heavy cream
1 teaspoon salt
½ teaspoon freshly ground black pepper
¼ teaspoon freshly grated nutmeg

(continued)

Melt 1 tablespoon butter in a large skillet over moderate heat. Add spinach and cook, tossing gently, until wilted and bright green. Drain in a colander and reserve.

Melt remaining 2 tablespoons butter in same skillet over moderate heat. Cook onion until soft, but not brown. Meanwhile chop spinach finely and add to onions. Add cream, bring to a boil, and cook until mixture thickens slightly, about 5 minutes. Stir in seasonings and serve immediately.

Roasted Eggplant and Sesame

This puree, also known as baba ghanoush, is great as a dip with pita triangles or garlic Naan (page 69). For lunch, we spread it on Grilled Chicken Sandwiches (page 63).

4 to 6 servings

1¾ pounds eggplant
2 tablespoons tahini (page 235)
1 tablespoon fresh lemon juice
1 tablespoon extra virgin olive oil
1 tablespoon pureed garlic (page 236)
1 teaspoon cayenne pepper
dash of Tabasco
salt and freshly ground black pepper to taste

Preheat broiler. Place eggplant on a baking sheet and broil, turning occasionally, until charred all over and softened, about 40 minutes. Set aside to cool.

When cool enough to handle, peel eggplant and roughly chop, reserving liquid. Transfer to a large bowl. Mix in remaining ingredients and season to taste with salt and pepper. Serve chilled or at room temperature.

Fried Vegetables

Parsnip Chips

These crisp chips are similar to potato chips, only sweeter. The combination of starch and sugar in parsnips makes them perfect for frying.

6 servings

1½ pounds parsnips
1 quart peanut oil
salt to taste

Peel parsnips. Using a mandoline or food processor fitted with 2-millimeter slicing blade, cut into 1⁄16-inch slices, lengthwise.

Heat oil in a large stockpot or saucepan to deep-fry temperature (350°F). Fry parsnips, a handful at a time, until pale golden and crisp. Remove with a slotted spoon, drain on paper towels, and sprinkle with salt. Serve immediately or reserve a day or 2 in plastic bags.

Fried Spinach

We use this technique to fry other greens, such as cilantro and parsley. The key is to expose the fragile leaves to hot oil just long enough to extract the water and turn them bright green and crispy, just like chips. We love to surprise people and serve our crispy spinach in bowls at parties or as an accompaniment to any dish that is not heavily sauced.

6 servings

3 bunches spinach, stems removed
1 quart vegetable oil
salt to taste

Wash spinach leaves thoroughly and pat dry with paper towels. Heat oil in a large stockpot or saucepan to deep-fry temperature (350°F). Fry a small handful of leaves at a time, until crisp, about 30 seconds. (Stand as far away as possible, since the water in spinach is bound to cause some splattering.) Remove with a slotted spoon, drain on paper towels, and sprinkle with salt. Serve immediately or reserve up to 2 hours at room temperature.

Shoestring Fries

These thin little sticks are fully fried. It is important to remove them from the oil the moment they turn golden. They can burn within seconds.

6 servings

6 small baking potatoes
1 quart peanut oil
salt to taste

Peel potatoes. Using a mandoline or food processor fitted with a 6-millimeter julienne blade, cut into 1/16-inch julienne, or matchsticks. Place in a large bowl and rinse under cold running water until water runs clear. Drain and pat dry with paper towels.

Heat oil in a large stockpot or saucepan to deep-fry temperature (350°F). Fry potatoes, a handful at a time, until pale golden and crisp. Drain on paper towels and sprinkle with salt. Serve immediately or reserve up to 2 hours.

Onion Rings

*Beer batter gets lighter
and fluffier as it sits.
You can mix it as
much as a day in
advance.*

6 servings

1 cup all-purpose flour
¾ tablespoon granulated sugar
1 teaspoon salt
1 teaspoon baking powder
1 teaspoon cayenne pepper
1 cup beer, room temperature
3 large onions
1 quart peanut oil
salt to taste

Combine ¾ cup flour, sugar, salt, baking powder, and cayenne in a medium bowl. Add beer all at once and whisk until smooth. Cover with plastic wrap and set aside at room temperature at least an hour.

Peel onions and cut across width into ¼-inch slices. Separate slices to form individual rings.

When batter is ready, heat oil in a large saucepan to deep-fry temperature (350°F). Dust a handful of onion rings with flour, then dip into batter to coat evenly. Deep-fry until golden brown, being careful not to crowd the pan. Remove with slotted spoon, drain on paper towels, sprinkle with salt, and serve immediately.

Cool Greens

Parsley Salad with Garlic Vinaigrette

People are usually shocked to learn what the ingredients are in this special salad. Blanching garlic creates a wild and buttery flavor. Since parsley leaves are so durable, this is one of the few salads that can be dressed in advance. Parsley, by the way, is exceptionally high in vitamin C.

4 Servings

12 garlic cloves, peeled and thinly sliced
1 cup virgin olive oil
2 tablespoons fresh lemon juice
1 teaspoon salt
¼ teaspoon freshly ground black pepper
2 bunches curly parsley

Bring a small pot of water to a boil. Blanch garlic about 3 minutes and drain. Combine garlic with olive oil, lemon juice, salt, and pepper and whisk to combine.

Remove stems and wash and dry leaves. Place in a bowl, add dressing, and toss to coat evenly. Serve small portions as an accompaniment.

Curly Endive, Apple, and Gorgonzola Salad

This rich little salad is special enough to start a dinner party. Follow it with something simple like Portuguese Mussel and Cockle Stew (page 116) or Confit of Duck (page 103).

6 servings

3 small heads curly endive, preferably frissé
3 large Granny Smith apples
1½ cups heavy cream
¾ cup red wine vinegar
3 ounces Gorgonzola, crumbled
1½ teaspoon salt
¼ teaspoon freshly ground black pepper

Separate endive leaves and wash well in cold running water. Trim and discard stems, break leaves into bite-sized pieces, and pat dry. Set aside in a bowl.

Peel and core apples and cut into thin slices. In another bowl, combine remaining ingredients. Add apple slices to cream mixture. (The apples can now be reserved in the refrigerator as long as 4 hours.)

At serving time, pour apple and cream mixture onto endive. Toss well to coat and serve immediately.

Red Chard and Hazelnut Salad

This luxurious salad can be made even richer by adding marinated goat cheese, as in the variation below.

6 servings

2 bunches red chard, stems trimmed, washed and dried
¼ cup roasted, skinned, and chopped hazelnuts (page 236)
⅔ cup extra virgin olive oil
3 tablespoons sherry wine vinegar
¾ teaspoon salt
¼ teaspoon freshly ground black pepper

Stack red chard leaves, roll, and slice across width in fine julienne. Combine chard and hazelnuts in a bowl and toss. Whisk remaining ingredients together in a bowl to form a vinaigrette. Toss dressing with salad just before serving.

Variation: Top with rounds of marinated goat cheese for a main course lunch salad or elegant starter. We marinate a log soft, unripened goat cheese from France, like Montrachet, in enough olive oil to cover, along with whole garlic cloves, 1 tablespoon peppercorns, about 5 bay leaves, and fresh herbs such as parsley, mint, basil, thyme, oregano, chives, and rosemary. This mixture can sit at room temperature, in a covered container, as long as a month. The cheese will keep absorbing flavor. Place ½-inch-thick rounds over individual salads and serve.

Cole Slaw

We like our Cole Slaw
clean and refreshing,
without a hint of
mayonnaise. If the
quantity is too large,
you can cut the recipe
in half.

makes 6 cups

1 large or 2 small green cabbages, about 2 pounds
1 cup vegetable oil
¼ cup granulated sugar
⅓ cup white vinegar
1 tablespoon stone-ground mustard
1 tablespoon celery seeds
1½ tablespoons grated horseradish, preferably fresh
1 teaspoon salt
¼ teaspoon freshly ground black pepper

Cut cabbage in quarters, lengthwise. Remove and discard cores and slice as finely as possible across width. Reserve in a large bowl.

Combine remaining ingredients in another bowl. Add, half a cup at a time, to shredded cabbage just until well moistened. You don't want a pool of dressing at bottom of bowl. Toss well and store in refrigerator.

Limestone Lettuce Salad

This dressing—stronger than most—is a unique combination of ethnic ingredients. It stands up well to any strong-tasting vegetable.

8 to 10 servings

6 small heads limestone lettuce or other greens

1 large carrot, peeled

2 pickling cucumbers or Kirbies (page 234), peeled

1 small daikon radish

DRESSING

2 tablespoons Thai Fish Sauce (page 235)

1 tablespoon fresh lemon juice

1 tablespoon rice wine vinegar (page 234)

2 tablespoons vegetable oil

1 tablespoon soy sauce

1 tablespoon Pernod

2 tablespoons sesame oil

2 teaspoons finely grated fresh ginger (page 235)

Thoroughly wash and dry lettuce. Break into bite-sized pieces and place in a large salad bowl. Julienne-slice carrot, cucumbers, and radish, and toss with greens.

Whisk dressing ingredients together in a bowl. Toss with salad just before serving.

Broccoli with Peanut Vinaigrette

*This easy green salad
won't wilt. A good
choice for a picnic.*

6 servings

4½ cups broccoli florets
½ cup roasted, unsalted peanuts
½ cup olive oil
¼ cup red wine vinegar
½ cup water
½ teaspoon salt
⅛ teaspoon freshly ground black pepper

Bring a medium saucepan of salted water to a boil. Blanch broccoli about 3 minutes. Immediately refresh in a bowl of iced water and drain.

Grind nuts in a blender or food processor until fine, being careful not to overprocess. Whisk nuts with remaining ingredients in a bowl until a vinaigrette is formed. Add broccoli, toss, and serve. The tossed salad may be stored in refrigerator for 6 to 8 hours.

Watercess and Avocado Salad

*With its bitter bite,
watercress is a good foil
for rich foods. This is
the salad we serve
beneath Warm Shredded
Chicken Salad (page
131) and Marinated
Scallops (page 19).*

6 servings

½ cup extra virgin olive oil
2 tablespoons fresh lemon juice
¾ teaspoon salt
¼ teaspoon freshly ground black pepper
5 large bunches watercress, stems removed, leaves washed and well
   dried
2 ripe avocados, halved, seeded, and peeled

Whisk together olive oil, lemon juice, salt, and pepper in a bowl. Tear watercress into bite-sized pieces and toss with dressing. Divide salad among 6 serving plates. Thinly slice avocado halves into strips lengthwise. Garnish center of each salad with avocado and serve.

City Cucumber Salad

This refreshing summer salad is a lovely accompaniment to a simple meal of grilled fish or chicken.

4 to 6 servings

6 cucumbers or 15 pickling cucumbers or Kirbies (page 234), peeled and trimmed

2 large ripe tomatoes

½ cup extra virgin olive oil

¼ cup red wine vinegar

1 teaspoon salt

½ teaspoon freshly ground black pepper

1 medium red onion, diced

Cut cucumbers in half lengthwise. Slice across width in ¼-inch pieces. (If using large cucumbers, remove seeds. They can remain in pickling cucumbers.) Cut tomatoes in half across width. Remove seeds and roughly chop.

Mix oil, vinegar, salt, and pepper together in a large bowl. Add chopped tomatoes, cucumbers, and onion. Toss well and chill as long as 6 hours.

Hot Greens

Sautéed Okra with Cumin

The key to keeping okra fresh-tasting is to wipe it clean with a damp cloth, then cook quickly, before it has a chance to absorb too much liquid and get gummy.

6 servings

6 tablespoons (¾ stick) unsalted butter
1½ pounds okra, stems trimmed, washed
1 teaspoon salt
½ teaspoon freshly ground black pepper
1½ teaspoons ground cumin

Melt butter over high heat in a medium sauté pan. Sauté okra with all seasonings 2 to 3 minutes. Reduce heat to moderate and cook, stirring occasionally, an additional 5 minutes. Serve hot.

Rapini with Garlic and Soy

Rapini is leafier and more pungent than ordinary broccoli. This simple preparation is delicious with either one.

6 servings

6 tablespoons (¾ stick) unsalted butter
2 tablespoons puréed garlic (page 236)
1½ pounds rapini or broccoli, peeled and roughly chopped
2 tablespoons soy sauce

Melt butter in a medium skillet over medium-low heat. Cook garlic gently to release oils but not to brown, about 3 minutes. Add rapini and cook over moderate heat until bright green, about 2 to 4 minutes. Stir in soy sauce and serve immediately.

Braised White Cabbage

Warm, tender cabbage
enriched with butter is
a comforting
accompaniment to
wintery dishes like Beef
Brisket (page 77).

6 servings

1 large head white cabbage
1 cup dry white wine
2 bay leaves
1½ teaspoons salt
¼ teaspoon freshly ground black pepper
8 tablespoons (1 stick) unsalted butter, cold

Preheat oven to 450°F. Cut cabbage in quarters, remove core, and shred finely.

Place wine and bay leaves in a large heavy saucepan. Bring to a boil and reduce by half. Add cabbage, salt, and pepper, and bring back to a boil. Cover with a tight-fitting lid and transfer to oven. Bake 30 to 35 minutes, until cabbage is thoroughly limp. Check pot after about 15 minutes and stir down cabbage.

Break butter into small pieces and stir into warm cabbage. Adjust seasonings and serve immediately or reheat in a 350°F oven 15 minutes.

Sautéed Mustard Greens

You can use this technique for collard, beet, or dandelion greens. Speed is essential, so the vegetables remain bright, flavorful, and full of vitamins. We like to serve this as an accompaniment with several dishes, such as Fried Egg Sandwich with Canadian Bacon (page 60) and Grilled Swordfish with Mustard (page 106).

6 servings

4 bunches mustard greens
2 tablespoons unsalted butter
½ teaspoon salt
½ teaspoon freshly ground black pepper

Trim greens of any tough stems. Wash and dry.

Roll leaves into a tight, long cylinder and cut across roll in ¼-inch slices.

Melt butter in a medium sauté pan over high heat. Sauté greens with salt and pepper just until wilted, about 2 to 3 minutes. Serve immediately.

Peapods with Ginger and Soy

Here is a simple, fast side dish that most people love.

6 servings

¾ pound Chinese snow peas or snap peas
4½ tablespoons unsalted butter
4 teaspoons freshly grated ginger (page 235)
4 teaspoons soy sauce
⅛ teaspoon freshly ground black pepper

Trim peapods of any strings or tough ends. Heat butter in a medium skillet over high heat. Sauté peapods until they begin to soften, about 2 minutes. Add ginger, soy sauce, and pepper. Toss lightly and serve immediately.

Sautéed Spinach with Parmesan Cheese

It takes only 3 minutes to prepare this lush dish. Though we are not miniature vegetable fans, baby spinach tastes wonderful prepared this way.

6 servings

3 bunches spinach
1½ tablespoons unsalted butter
1½ tablespoons pureed garlic (page 236)
¾ teaspoon salt
¼ teaspoon freshly ground black pepper
2 small tomatoes, peeled, seeded, and diced (page 236)
1¼ cups freshly grated Parmesan cheese

Thoroughly wash and dry spinach and remove stems.

Melt butter in a medium skillet over moderate heat. Sauté garlic about a second. Add spinach and stir until evenly wilted, about 2 minutes. Add salt, pepper, and tomatoes. Cook an additional minute. Stir in grated Parmesan, remove from heat, taste and adjust seasonings. Serve immediately. If spinach releases too much water, you can drain mixture in a colander before serving. Taste and adjust seasonings again after draining.

Leeks with Caraway

In this satisfying side
dish, savory leeks are
cooked just long enough
to lose their crunch and
become enriched with
butter and wine.

6 servings

6 leeks
4 tablespoons (½ stick) unsalted butter
2 tablespoons caraway seeds, chopped
1 teaspoon salt
½ teaspoon freshly ground black pepper
½ cup dry white wine

Trim roots and dark green portion of leeks. Cut in half length-wise and wash thoroughly under cold running water. Cut into ¼-inch diagonal slices, across width.

Melt butter in a medium skillet over medium-high heat. Add leeks, caraway, salt, and pepper, and cook until leeks are soft, about 2 minutes. Add wine, reduce heat to low and cook, covered, 3 to 5 minutes. Serve immediately.

Shredded Brussels Sprouts

This sweet, crunchy vegetable is always a surprise to people who ordinarily hate Brussels sprouts. Guaranteed to convert even the most determined detractor.

6 to 8 servings

1½ pounds Brussels sprouts
4 tablespoons (½ stick) unsalted butter
½ teaspoon salt
¼ teaspoon freshly ground black pepper
2 teaspoons water
juice of ½ lime

Soak whole sprouts in a large bowl of cold, salted water to clean. Then trim and discard ends and any bitter outer leaves. Cut each in half lengthwise, then slice thinly across width.

Melt butter in a large skillet over medium-high heat. Sauté sprouts with salt and pepper until they start to brown. Add water and cook until barely limp, about 4 minutes. (The water changes the action from sautéeing to steaming.) Stir in lime juice and serve immediately.

Vegetable Combinations

Sweet and Sour Red Cabbage

Although it can be eaten hot or cold, the flavor of this sweet and sour accompaniment benefits from a few days in the refrigerator. We use it to garnish almost anything: sandwiches, smoked fish, pâtés, salads, brisket, pork, or even liver. And it can always be found at Thanksgiving at Mary Sue's mom's house.

10 to 12 servings

1 large head red cabbage
2 large onions, thinly sliced
½ cup granulated sugar
1 cup red wine vinegar
1 tablespoon caraway seeds
1 bay leaf
1½ teaspoons salt
¼ teaspoon freshly ground black pepper
½ cup rendered duck fat (page 236), preferably, or clarified butter (page 235)

Cut cabbage in quarters, core, and finely julienne. Combine all ingredients, except the fat, in a large bowl. Stir to blend.

Heat fat in a large heavy skillet or Dutch oven over moderate heat. Add cabbage mixture and reduce heat to a simmer. Cover and cook, stirring occasionally, until cabbage is tender, about 1 hour. Serve hot or cold. Sweet and sour cabbage may be stored in refrigerator up to 5 days and may also be reheated.

Roasted Onion Compote

Sweet white onions with cream and bacon are irresistible, especially with a holiday dinner of turkey or roast beef. You can make this dish the day before and reheat with no loss of flavor.

6 servings

1¾ pounds small white onions, with skins
½ pound thickly sliced bacon
½ cup brandy
1½ cups heavy cream
½ teaspoon freshly ground black pepper

Preheat oven to 350°F. Arrange onions in an even layer on a large baking sheet. Bake, shaking pan occasionally to ensure even roasting, about 40 minutes. The largest onion should feel soft when pressed. Set aside to cool. Trim ends and peel.

Slice bacon across width into ¼-inch pieces. Fry until crisp in a large skillet. Drain off half fat, leaving bacon in pan. Remove from heat. Pour in brandy, return to burner, turn heat to high, and light alcohol with a match. When flame subsides, add cream, reserved onions, and pepper. Cook until cream is reduced by half. Serve immediately.

Sweet and Sour Eggplant

This hearty eggplant dish goes well with simple grilled foods or a roast, like Herb-Stuffed Leg of Lamb with Pimento Sauce (page 79).

6 servings

3½ pounds eggplant, preferably Japanese
1 tablespoon coarse salt
1 cup olive oil
2 large onions, diced
2 tablespoons pureed garlic (page 236)
1½ tablespoons tomato paste
½ cup red wine vinegar
⅓ cup capers with juice
½ cup brown sugar
salt and Tabasco to taste

Trim ends of eggplants. Cut across width into ¼-inch slices, leaving skins on. (If you are using regular eggplants, cut into quarters lengthwise before slicing.) Place in a colander, sprinkle with coarse salt and let sweat 30 minutes. Pat dry with paper towels.

Heat oil in a large skillet over high heat. Sauté eggplant in batches until lightly brown, about 1 minute per side. Set aside to drain on paper towels.

In same pan, sauté onions until golden. Reduce heat, add garlic, and cook just long enough to release its aroma. Add tomato paste and cook 2 minutes. Stir in remaining ingredients. Continue cooking another 3 minutes. Taste to adjust seasonings. Serve immediately or chill a minimum of 2 hours or up to 2 days.

City Ratatouille

In our ratatouille, the vegetables are neatly diced, then sautéed individually so each retains its own distinctive flavor.

6 servings

1 medium eggplant, with skin
1 large zucchini, with skin
1 yellow crookneck squash, with skin
3 bell peppers, preferably red, yellow, and green, seeded
1 large onion
1 cup olive oil
2 teaspoons pureed garlic (page 236)
1 cup kalamata olives, cut from pit in slices
5 bay leaves
1 teaspoon chopped fresh thyme
1 teaspoon chopped fresh oregano
1 teaspoon salt
½ teaspoon freshly ground black pepper
1 cup Brown Lamb Stock (page 57) or chicken stock or tomato juice
2 large tomatoes, peeled, seeded, and diced (page 236)

Trim ends and cores of eggplant, zucchini, yellow squash, and peppers. Cut each into ½-inch dice. Reserve separately. Trim end of onion and cut into ½-inch dice.

Place a large heavy skillet over high heat to heat dry pan. When you add oil, it should heat immediately. First, sauté eggplant until golden. Remove with a slotted spoon and reserve on paper towels. Then sauté zucchini and crookneck squash until golden and set aside to drain.

Reduce heat to moderate. In same pan, cook onions until soft and translucent. Add bell peppers and garlic, and cook until peppers soften, about 2 minutes. Add olives, bay leaves, thyme, oregano, salt, and pepper. Cook an additional minute.

Add Brown Lamb Stock, tomatoes, and reserved vegetables. Simmer, uncovered, about 5 minutes. Remove and discard bay leaves and serve hot or chilled.

Spaghetti Squash and Tomato Sauté

*Tomatoes bring out the
acidity of this lovely
crunchy squash. This
goes with just about
everything.*

6 servings

1 spaghetti squash, about 2 pounds
4 tablespoons (½ stick) unsalted butter
1½ teaspoons salt
½ teaspoon freshly ground black pepper
1 tomato, peeled, seeded, and diced (page 236)

Preheat oven to 350°F. Cut squash in half lengthwise and re-move and discard inner seeds. Coat insides with 1 tablespoon butter and sprinkle with ½ teaspoon salt. Place cut-side down in a roasting pan and add about an inch of boiling water. Cover with aluminum foil and bake 30 minutes. Set aside to cool.

When cool enough to handle, scoop out meat with a spoon, discarding skins. Fluff hot strands with a fork to separate.

Melt remaining 3 tablespoons butter in a large skillet over medium-high heat. Sauté squash with remaining salt and pepper about 5 minutes. Add tomato and cook briefly, to evenly heat. Serve immediately.

Condiments

Horseradish and Mustard and Mayonnaise

The perfect sandwich spread. We use it on practically everything.

6 servings

1 cup Mayonnaise (page 179)
½ cup freshly grated horseradish
½ cup Dijon or stone-ground mustard
freshly ground black pepper to taste

Mix ingredients together and season to taste with pepper.

Pantry Pickles

Susan's mother's recipe for homemade pickles takes about 20 minutes from start to finish. (You can use a food processor for the slicing.)

makes 1 generous quart

6 pickling cucumbers or Kirbies (page 234), with skins
1 onion, thinly sliced across the width
1 red bell pepper, cored, seeded, and julienned
2 cups rice wine vinegar (page 234)
½ cup granulated sugar
1 tablespoon coarse salt

Cut cucumbers across width into ¹⁄₁₆-inch slices, diagonally. Combine all ingredients in a medium saucepan. Bring to a boil, reduce to a simmer, and cook, uncovered, 10 to 15 minutes. Store in pickling liquid, in refrigerator.

Variation: Add diced red, yellow, and green bell peppers for canned Christmas gifts.

Mayonnaise

Question: How do you hold the bowl, pour in the oil, and whisk all at the same time?

Answer: Gather a damp towel snugly around the bowl's bottom. The towel will keep the bowl still—or at least on the counter.

makes 1½ cups

2 egg yolks
1 teaspoon red wine vinegar
juice of ½ lemon
½ teaspoon salt
¼ teaspoon freshly ground black pepper
dash of Tabasco
dash of Worcestershire sauce
1 cup vegetable oil

In a bowl, combine egg yolks, vinegar, lemon juice, salt, pepper, Tabasco, and Worcestershire. Blend with a whisk. Gradually add oil, a drop a time, whisking constantly. As mixture begins to thicken and looks more like mayonnaise, you can add oil more generously. Adjust seasonings and store in refrigerator as long as 4 days.

Hamburger Relish

This is another
wonderful Ruthie
Feniger recipe.

makes 1 quart

3 ripe tomatoes, peeled and seeded (page 236)

¼ head green cabbage, cored

2 small green bell peppers, seeds removed

2 medium onions

1 quart white vinegar

1¼ cups granulated sugar

2 teaspoons Dijon mustard

1 teaspoon celery seeds

1 teaspoon ground cloves

1 teaspoon cinnamon

½ tablespoon turmeric

Place tomatoes, cabbage, peppers, and onions in a food processor fitted with steel blade and pulse until roughly chopped, or dice vegetables by hand.

Combine remaining ingredients in a large saucepan and bring to a boil. Add chopped vegetables, bring back to a boil, and reduce to a simmer. Cook, uncovered, until thick, about 1 hour. Relish keeps in refrigerator about 3 weeks.

Homemade Yogurt

1 quart milk
1 cup half and half
1 tablespoon plain yogurt

Combine milk and half and half in a medium saucepan. Bring to a boil over low heat. Remove from heat and transfer to a clean bowl. Set aside to cool to 115°F. Add yogurt and vigorously whisk.

Cover bowl with plastic wrap, then wrap well with heavy towels or a blanket. Set aside in a warm place for 6 to 8 hours, or longer according to taste. The longer yogurt sits, the more acidic it will become. Store in sealed containers in refrigerator.

Three Raitas

A raita is a natural accompaniment to any of our curries. They are all derived from Indian cuisine, where these flavored, textured yogurts provide a break from the spicier tastes of the meal. Each is distinctive: The banana is sweet and crunchy. The cucumber is the most refreshing. (Try increasing the proportion of cucumbers to yogurt for a salad.) And, the smoky eggplant is substantial enough to serve as a vegetable side dish.

makes 1½ cups

Banana Raita

2 tablespoons black mustard seeds (page 232)
1 large ripe banana
¼ cup fresh, or dry, unsweetened, grated coconut
1 cup plain yogurt
pinch of salt and freshly ground black pepper

Place seeds in a small dry sauté pan and cook over moderate heat until seeds turn gray and start popping. Remove from heat.

Coarsely mash banana in a medium bowl. Add mustard seeds, grated coconut, yogurt, salt, and pepper. Stir to combine and serve at room temperature or chilled. May be stored in the refrigerator about a day.

Cucumber Raita

1½ teaspoons olive oil
2 teaspoons pureed garlic (page 236)
2 teaspoons ground cumin
2 pickling cucumbers or Kirbies (page 234), with skins, finely diced
½ cup plain yogurt
¼ bunch cilantro, stems removed, chopped
¼ teaspoon salt
pinch of freshly ground black pepper
2 dashes of Tabasco

Heat oil in a small skillet over moderate heat. Cook garlic, stirring occasionally, until aroma is released, about 2 minutes. Add cumin and cook briefly, just to combine flavors. Remove from heat.

Transfer to medium bowl. Add remaining ingredients and stir to combine. Serve at room temperature or chilled.

makes 1 cup

Eggplant Raita

1 small eggplant
1 teaspoon olive oil
1 tablespoon pureed garlic (page 236)
1 tomato, with skin, seeded and diced
½ bunch cilantro, stems removed, chopped
1 cup plain yogurt
½ teaspoon salt
pinch of freshly ground black pepper

Preheat broiler and place tray as far as possible from flame. Place eggplant on a baking sheet and roast, turning occasionally, until charred on all sides and thoroughly soft, about 45 minutes. Set aside to cool.

Heat oil in a small skillet over moderate heat. Cook garlic, stirring occasionally, until aroma is released, about 2 minutes. Transfer to a medium bowl along with tomato, cilantro, yogurt, salt, and pepper. Hold eggplant over and squeeze juices into bowl. Peel and finely chop eggplant. Add to yogurt mixture, stir well, and serve at room temperature or chilled.

makes 2½ cups

Sauerkraut

Here's a well-kept secret: Sauerkraut is incredibly easy to make. Just combine the ingredients and wait 5 days—no cooking needed!

makes 4 cups

1 (3½-pound) green cabbage
3 tablespoons coarse salt

Cut cabbage into quarters and remove core. With a mandoline or food processor fitted with a 2-millimeter slicing blade, slice as thinly as possible. Place in a large bowl with salt and toss to combine.

Transfer to a large glass or ceramic container and tap down by hand so liquid rises to top. Cover with a damp towel touching cabbage and top with a 3-pound weight. Cover again with a layer of plastic wrap and set aside in a warm place 5 days to ferment. Sauerkraut may be kept in a sealed container in refrigerator as long as 3 weeks.

Curry Popcorn

We keep huge bowls of this bright orange popcorn around at all times. You will want to adjust the spices to taste—this is definitely spicy!

makes 12 cups

½ teaspoon cayenne pepper
½ teaspoon ground cumin
½ teaspoon turmeric
1 teaspoon cracked black peppercorns (page 235)
1 teaspoon salt
¼ cup vegetable oil
½ cup unpopped popcorn

Measure spices onto a plate and place near stove.

Place oil and one kernel popcorn in a pot on a burner. Turn heat to high, cover pot, and cook until kernel pops. Then add popcorn and cover again. When corn starts popping, quickly add spices. Cover and cook, shaking constantly, until the popping stops.

Be careful not to breathe in the spiced fumes as they can burn your throat.

Marinated Mushrooms

Mushrooms are great for marinating. They are as absorbent as sponges! Keep these on hand for salads, sandwiches, and easy hors d'oeuvres.

makes 3 cups

1 pound large white mushrooms, stems removed

MARINADE

1 cup olive oil

½ cup fresh lemon juice

2 shallots, chopped

1 teaspoon pureed garlic (page 236)

1 teaspoon dry mustard

½ teaspoon cracked black peppercorns (page 235)

¼ teaspoon ground ginger

1 bay leaf

1 teaspoon salt

Clean mushrooms by washing briefly under cold running water. Carefully pat dry with paper towels.

Combine marinade ingredients in a large bowl. Add mushrooms and toss to evenly coat. Transfer to a container and press mushrooms down until the liquid rises to top. Cover with plastic wrap and a heavy weight, and refrigerate 2 to 5 days.

Applesauce

We love the crunch and bite of Granny Smith apples for homemade applesauce. Delicious with short ribs or potato pancakes, of course.

makes 3 cups

6 green apples, peeled, cored, and cut into chunks

1½ cups water

1 cup granulated sugar

⅓ cup fresh lemon juice

Combine ingredients in a large heavy saucepan. Cover and bring to a boil. Reduce heat to a simmer and cook until apples are soft, about ½ hour. Remove from heat and stir with a wooden spoon or whisk until texture suits your taste. Chill.

Dill Pickles

If you like pickled vegetables, try substituting small onions, carrots, and cauliflower for the cucumbers.

makes 15 pickles

15 pickling cucumbers or Kirbies (page 234)

PICKLING LIQUID

3 cups water

2 cups white vinegar

¼ cup coarse salt

2 tablespoons granulated sugar

¾ teaspoon ground cumin

½ teaspoon ground ginger

1 teaspoon black peppercorns

½ teaspoon turmeric

2 whole cloves

1 bay leaf

1 medium onion, sliced

1 celery stalk, sliced

½ carrot, peeled and sliced

1 jalapeño pepper, sliced with seeds

8 garlic cloves, peeled

1 bunch dill

1 sprig thyme

Bring a large stockpot water to a boil. Add cucumbers, immediately remove from heat, and drain in a colander. Rinse with cold water and reserve.

Combine pickling liquid ingredients in a medium saucepan and bring to a boil. Place cucumbers in a large container with remaining vegetables and herbs. Pour hot pickling liquid over cucumber mixture and let cool. Tap down solids until liquid rises to top. Cover with plastic wrap and let stand at room temperature 1 day. Transfer to a sealed container and refrigerate 3 days before serving. Store indefinitely.

Spicy Apple Chutney

This sweet chutney is delicious with curries or as a spread for breakfast toast. If you are a chutney fan, see Mint and Cilantro Chutney (page 5) and Tamarind Chutney (page 74) for more ideas.

makes 3 cups

4 green apples
2 tablespoons vegetable oil
1 tablespoon mustard seeds
1 medium onion, diced
1 red bell pepper, cored and diced
1 teaspoon salt
2 teaspoons pureed garlic (page 236)
1 serrano chile, diced with seeds
1 teaspoon ground ginger
1 teaspoon ground allspice
¼ cup raisins
1 cup packed brown sugar
¾ cup red wine vinegar
1 cup water

Peel apples and cut into quarters. Remove cores, roughly chop, and reserve.

Heat oil in a large saucepan over high heat. Add mustard seeds, cover, and cook until popping stops. Reduce heat and add onion, red pepper, and salt. Cook, uncovered, stirring occasionally, until onions are translucent. Stir in garlic, serrano chile, ginger, and allspice, and cook an additional minute.

Add remaining ingredients, including reserved apples. Cook, uncovered, over moderate heat, until mixture is soft and aromatic, about 40 minutes. Chill before serving.

Pickled Tomatoes

Packed into attractive jars, these extremely potent, sweet and spicy tomatoes make lovely Christmas gifts. We serve small ramekins of this Indian dish with Spicy City Chicken (page 97) and on vegetarian platters.

makes 3 cups or 6 side dishes

1½ pounds tomatoes, peeled (page 236)
1 bunch scallions, white and green, sliced
3 to 5 serrano chiles, with seeds, sliced
¾ cup white vinegar
¼ cup brown sugar
1 tablespoon coarse salt
2 tablespoons freshly grated ginger (page 235)
2 tablespoons pureed garlic (page 236)
1 tablespoon black or yellow mustard seeds (page 232)
1 tablespoon cracked black peppercorns (page 235)
1 tablespoon ground cumin
2 teaspoons cayenne pepper
1 teaspoon turmeric
¾ cup olive oil

Slice tomatoes into 6 wedges each. Reserve in a large bowl with scallions and serrano chiles.

In a medium saucepan bring vinegar to a boil. Add sugar and salt, and cook until dissolved, about 1 minute. Remove from heat and reserve.

Measure ginger, garlic, mustard seeds, cracked peppercorns, cumin, cayenne, and turmeric onto a plate and place near stove. In another medium saucepan heat oil over moderate heat until smoking. Add spices and cook, stirring constantly with a wooden spoon, until aromas are released, about 2 minutes. Remove from heat and stir in vinegar mixture.

Immediately pour over reserved vegetables. Mix well, cover with plastic wrap, and refrigerate a minimum of 3 days.

6 Desserts and Beverages

Everyone seems to crave something sweet after a meal—be it a simple fruit tart or an extravagant chocolate cake—and so do we.

Since baking was Mary Sue's first love—she worked at a pastry shop for five years while attending chef's school—she has a few suggestions for home bakers. The trick to overcoming nervousness is to repeat recipes. Rather than try a new dessert each time you give a dinner party, master two or three favorites. Develop your confidence before going on to something new. Make the dessert in advance, away from the storm and strife of last-minute preparations. Remember, your guests will always be impressed by something fresh—however humble.

Chocolate

Black Velvet

This sophisticated cake is dense with ground nuts and whiskey. With its shiny top coat and feathery white lines, this glamorous chocolate cake is a good choice for a grownup's birthday party.

12 servings

14 ounces semisweet chocolate, chopped

1 cup (2 sticks) unsalted butter, softened

¼ cup water

½ cup plus 2 tablespoons finely ground hazelnuts, with skins

½ cup plus 2 tablespoons finely ground almonds, with skins

½ cup plus 2 tablespoons pastry flour

6 eggs, separated

1⅓ cups granulated sugar

½ cup good Scotch whiskey

Ganache, recipe follows

Pure White Frosting, recipe follows

Preheat oven to 325°F. Butter and flour a 10-inch springform pan and line with parchment paper.

Melt chocolate in the top of a double boiler or in a bowl over simmering water and remove from heat. Add butter, a tablespoon at a time, stirring until smooth. Stir in water.

Combine hazelnuts, almonds, and flour in bowl and set aside.

With an electric mixer, beat yolks at medium speed until light and fluffy. Gradually add sugar, beating until very light. With a wooden spoon, gently fold into chocolate mixture.

Fold reserved nut mixture and Scotch whiskey into chocolate mixture in three stages, alternating ingredients.

In a clean bowl, whisk egg whites until soft peaks form. Gently fold into batter in two parts.

Spread evenly in prepared pan and tap on a counter to eliminate air pockets. Bake 45 to 50 minutes, or until a toothpick inserted in center comes out slightly moist. (The top may be cracked and the center wobbly.) Set aside to cool, in pan on rack, about 1 hour. Chill a minimum of 3 hours, preferably overnight.

Release and remove sides of pan. Invert onto a parchment- or wax paper-coated counter or cake decorating table. Prepare Ganache and Pure White Frosting.

Pour Ganache over cold cake. Let it set a few seconds, then, using a cake spatula, spread evenly over top and sides.

Fill a pastry bag fitted with your finest tip, or a handmade paper cone with a closed tip, with Pure White Frosting. Quickly draw parallel lines, ¾-inch apart, across Ganache. Drag tip of a sharp paring knife through lines at 1-inch intervals, in a perpendicular fashion. Turn cake around and draw knife through white lines in opposite direction. The resulting pattern should be a feathery checkerboard of wavy white lines.

GANACHE

6 ounces semisweet chocolate, chopped

¾ cup heavy cream

makes 1½ cups

Place chocolate in a medium bowl. Bring cream to a boil. Pour into chocolate and stir until chocolate is completely melted. Let cool until mixture is less than body temperature.

PURE WHITE FROSTING

⅔ cup confectioners' sugar

1 tablespoon milk

makes ½ cup

Mix in a small bowl until smooth.

Cupcakes Hostess Style

Hostess cupcakes are our madeleines—one whiff and we are transported to childhood. While we improved the taste, the appearance remains classic Hostess. Milk is still the perfect accompaniment.

This is our favorite chocolate cake recipe. Use it for delicious layer cakes, with softened cream cheese and confectioners' sugar or whipped cream and sliced bananas, perhaps, between the layers.

For the best, moistest cupcakes, we bake them in ¼-inch-thick stoneware coffee cups.

makes 18 cupcakes

5 ounces unsweetened bitter chocolate, chopped
1 cup packed brown sugar
1 cup milk
4 egg yolks
8 tablespoons (1 stick) unsalted butter, softened
1 cup granulated sugar
2 cups all-purpose flour
1 teaspoon salt
1 teaspoon baking soda
¼ cup heavy cream
1 teaspoon vanilla extract
3 egg whites
1 recipe Pastry Cream (page 218)
½ recipe Ganache (page 191)
1 recipe Pure White Frosting (page 191)

Preheat oven to 325°F. Butter and flour a 12-cup and a 6-cup muffin tin.

Melt chocolate in the top of a double boiler or in a bowl over simmering water. In another bowl, combine brown sugar, ½ cup milk, and 2 egg yolks. Whisk until combined. Add to melted chocolate and stir constantly (while cooking over simmering water) until mixture is shiny and thick, about 3 minutes. Set aside to cool.

In a clean bowl, cream butter and granulated sugar until light. Add remaining 2 egg yolks, one at a time, beating well after each addition.

In another bowl, mix together flour, salt, and baking soda.

Combine cream, vanilla extract, and remaining ½ cup milk in a small bowl and reserve.

Pour cooled chocolate mixture into creamed butter and sugar. Whisk until smooth. Add combined dry ingredients and cream mixture in three stages, alternating liquid and dry ingredients, and ending with liquid.

Beat egg whites until soft peaks form. Gently fold, all at once, into batter. Spoon batter into muffin cups, about two-thirds full.

Bake 20 to 25 minutes, until a toothpick inserted in center comes out clean. Set aside to cool, in pan on rack, about 10 minutes. Invert and set aside on a lined sheet pan to cool, about an hour. Prepare Pastry Cream, Ganache, and Pure White Frosting.

Using the tip of a small paring knife, cut a small cone from bottom of each cupcake. Reserve cones. Scoop out about 1 teaspoon cake from center of each cupcake. Fill a pastry bag fitted with a plain tip with Pastry Cream. Pipe cream into cupcakes, then replace reserved cones. Place bottom-side down on a lined sheet pan and chill.

When Ganache is room temperature, dip cupcakes in to coat tops. Fill a plain-tipped pastry bag with Pure White Frosting and decorate with a squiggle across each top, Hostess style. Store in refrigerator until serving time.

Variation: For a layer cake, fill 2 buttered and floured 10-inch round pans and bake for 25 to 35 minutes, until a toothpick inserted in center comes out clean. Fill with softened cream cheese whipped with confectioners' sugar or with whipped cream and bananas.

City Chocolate with Espresso Crème Anglaise

This sweet chocolate pâte works like a magnet to attract chocolate lovers. A good choice for an elegant dinner party, it can be put together quickly and reserved in the refrigerator as long as 4 days.

14 servings

3 tablespoons brandy
½ cup golden raisins
1 pound 2 ounces semisweet chocolate
1¾ cups (3½ sticks) unsalted butter
10 eggs, separated
Espresso Crème Anglaise, recipe follows

Line a 12½ × 4½-inch sharp-edged loaf pan with enough aluminum foil to hang over sides about 3 inches. Combine brandy and raisins in a small saucepan and warm over low heat. Reserve.

Chop chocolate into small pieces and melt with butter in the top of a double boiler or in a bowl over simmering water. Remove from heat and stir in reserved raisins and brandy. Whisk in yolks until combined.

Whisk egg whites until soft peaks form. Gently fold whites into chocolate mixture in two stages.

Pour into prepared pan, tap on counter to remove air gaps, smooth top, and cover with plastic wrap touching top. Chill 6 hours or overnight.

To serve, remove plastic wrap and invert onto a serving platter. The chocolate should release easily. Remove aluminum foil.

Coat dessert plates with Espresso Crème Anglaise. Top each with a slice of chocolate. This slices most easily with a long, thin knife that has been dipped into hot water.

Espresso Crème Anglaise

    8 egg yolks
    1 cup granulated sugar
    2 cups milk
    1½ tablespoons finely ground coffee
    1 teaspoon vanilla extract

In a large bowl, whisk together egg yolks and sugar. Line a sieve with a paper coffee filter. Combine milk and coffee in a medium saucepan and bring to a boil.

Pour hot milk and coffee through sieve and into egg mixture, whisking constantly. Return to saucepan. Cook over moderate heat, stirring constantly, until the mixture thickens slightly and coats the back of a wooden spoon, about 5 minutes. Remove from heat. Stir in vanilla and chill.

Tarts and Pies

Tarte Tatin

This French country dessert is really an upside-down apple tart. The caramelized apples add a lovely deep brown color to this classic tart. A great winter dessert after a stew or braised meat dinner.

8 servings

12 red or golden delicious apples
2 cups granulated sugar
1 cup water
8 tablespoons (1 stick) unsalted butter
⅓ recipe **Pie Dough** (page 206) or 5 ounces puff pastry

Have ready an 8-inch round × 2½-inch deep sauté pan with straight sides and an ovenproof handle, or a *heavy* 8-inch cake pan. Peel apples, cut in half lengthwise, and remove cores.

Combine sugar and water in sauté pan. Cook over moderate heat until caramelized, about 15 minutes. Remove from heat. Using tongs, arrange a layer of apples upright and close together. Form a spiral with core sides touching curved sides from the center out. Fill pan as tightly as possible.

Cut butter into small pieces and sprinkle over apples in pan. Pile remaining apples, cut-side down, over butter. Cover with aluminum foil and place inside a 1- to 2-inch larger sauté pan (or roasting pan) to catch drippings.

Return to burner and cook over medium-low heat about 1 hour 20 minutes. Check pan every 20 minutes or so, pressing down apples on top. As apples cook, they shrink—eventually they will fit comfortably in pan. Also, pour any juices—as long as they're not burned—that spill into bottom pan back into apples. Set aside to cool about 15 minutes.

Preheat oven to 350°F.

On a lightly floured board, roll dough into a 9-inch circle, about ¼-inch thick. Let rest 15 minutes. Place over apples, allowing edges to hang over pan.

Bake about 35 minutes. Set aside to cool in pan ½ hour. Invert onto a serving platter and let sit, without lifting pan, 10 minutes. Remove pan and serve warm.

Pecan Tart

This traditional filling is so rich we like to serve it in a thin tart shell.

8 to 10 servings

½ recipe Pâte Sucrée (page 207)
3 eggs
¾ cup packed brown sugar
½ cup plus 1 teaspoon dark corn syrup
2 tablespoons honey
2 tablespoons molasses
6 tablespoons (¾ stick) unsalted butter, melted
2 teaspoons vanilla extract
1 teaspoon salt
2½ cups pecan halves

Preheat oven to 325°F.

Use a 10-inch tart pan with a removable bottom. Roll Pâte Sucrée to ⅛-inch thickness and line pan. Chill 15 minutes. Bake empty shell about 15 minutes. Meanwhile make filling.

In a large bowl, whisk together eggs, brown sugar, corn syrup, honey, molasses, butter, vanilla, and salt. Add pecans and mix to evenly coat.

Pour filling into prebaked tart shell and bake until center is set, 35 to 40 minutes. Set aside to cool on rack.

Lemon Hazelnut Tart

This is a sophisticated fruit tart. A dense cake layer is covered with lemon sections topped with a hazelnut-studded meringue. You can simplify the preparation by baking the cake a day in advance.

8 to 10 servings

1 cup finely ground hazelnuts
1 cup finely ground almonds
3 eggs, separated
¾ cup granulated sugar
grated zest of 1 lemon
1 teaspoon vanilla extract
1½ tablespoons all-purpose flour
¼ teaspoon salt
Meringue and Lemon Garnish, recipe follows

Preheat oven to 350°F. Line a 10-inch round cake pan with parchment paper, butter, and flour.

Mix together hazelnuts and almonds, and reserve.

In an electric mixer, with whisk attachment, whip egg yolks and sugar until pale yellow. Add lemon zest and vanilla. Mix until light and fluffy, and reserve.

In a small bowl, combine 1 cup ground nut mixture with flour and set aside. Reserve remaining cup for meringue.

In another bowl, beat egg whites until foamy. Sprinkle in salt and continue beating until soft peaks form. Fold alternating thirds nut-and-flour mixture and whites into beaten egg yolk mixture. Pour into prepared pan.

Bake 25 to 30 minutes until lightly browned. Set aside to cool, in pan on rack, about 10 minutes. Run a knife along inside edge to loosen, invert onto platter, and remove parchment. While cake is cooling, prepare garnish.

MERINGUE AND LEMON GARNISH

3 lemons
4 large egg whites
1¼ cups granulated sugar
1 cup reserved ground nut mixture
confectioners' sugar for garnish

Preheat oven to 300°F. Place cake layer on a baking sheet lined with parchment paper.

Slice ends off lemons and stand upright on a counter. Cut away skin and membrane, exposing fruit. Working over a bowl to catch the juice, separate sections by slicing with a serrated knife between membranes. Remove and discard seeds. Arrange sections evenly over cake and, using a small strainer, drizzle juice on top.

In a clean bowl of an electric mixer, whisk egg whites until foamy. Gradually add sugar, whisking continuously, until stiff peaks form. (It takes about 10 minutes of beating at high speed for the meringue to get shiny and thick.) Gently fold in reserved nuts.

Spread meringue evenly over cake and bake ½ hour. As meringue drys, it may start to crack—that's OK. Set aside to cool on rack. Dust with confectioners' sugar before serving.

Linzer Tart

This is a fantastic dough—packed with fresh citrus zest, spices, and a fair share of butter. If you have difficulty working with such a rich dough, return it to the refrigerator whenever it softens.

8 to 10 servings

1 cup (2 sticks) unsalted butter, softened
1 cup granulated sugar
2 egg yolks
grated zest of 1 lemon
grated zest of 1 orange
2½ cups all-purpose flour
1 cup finely ground hazelnuts
1 teaspoon baking powder
2 teaspoons cinnamon
½ teaspoon ground cloves
¼ teaspoon salt
1 cup good-quality raspberry preserves

To make dough, cream together butter and sugar until light and fluffy. Add egg yolks, lemon zest, and orange zest. Beat until well-combined.

In another bowl, mix together remaining ingredients, except preserves, of course. Add dry mixture all at once to creamed mixture and mix briefly, until just combined. (This dough looks more like cookie dough than pastry.) Wrap in plastic and chill until firm, about 4 hours or overnight.

Before rolling dough, preheat oven to 350°F.

Divide dough in half. On a generously floured board, briefly knead 1 piece dough and flatten with the palm of your hand. Gently roll dough to ¼-inch thickness and use to line a 9- or 10-inch tart pan with a removable bottom. This rich dough patches easily. Chill about 10 minutes.

Meanwhile, roll second piece dough to form a 12 × 4-inch rectangle. Using a sharp knife or pastry wheel, cut lengthwise strips, about ⅓-inch wide. Remove lined tart shell from refrigerator and spread evenly with raspberry preserves. To create a lattice pattern with pastry strips, first lay some strips in parallel lines, ½-inch apart. Press to edges of crust to seal. Then lay a second row of strips at a 45° angle to first. Press to crust to seal. (Save leftover dough for cookies.)

Bake 45 minutes, until crust is golden brown and filling bubbly in center. Set aside to cool.

Plum Streusel Tart

You can create an infinite variety of delicious fruit tarts with these basic components: Pâte Sucrée, Almond Cream, and Streusel. Along with this recipe come a few suggestions.

8 servings

½ recipe Pâte Sucrée (page 207)

ALMOND CREAM
½ cup plus 1 tablespoon granulated sugar
1 cup sliced almonds, blanched
9 tablespoons (1 stick plus 1 tablespoon) unsalted butter, softened
1 egg
1 egg yolk
2 tablespoons rum
1 teaspoon vanilla extract

To make Almond Cream, process sugar and almonds in a food processor until fine. Add butter, 1 tablespoon at a time, processing after each addition until smooth. Add remaining ingredients and process until smooth. Cover and refrigerate until ready to assemble. The Almond Cream may be made up to 4 days in advance.

STREUSEL
½ cup packed brown sugar
7 tablespoons unsalted butter, room temperature
1 teaspoon cinnamon
¼ teaspoon salt
1 cup plus 2 tablespoons all-purpose flour

(*continued*)

Cream together sugar and butter until smooth. Add cinnamon and salt, and mix until blended. Add flour. Mix with your fingers just until crumbly. Reserve.

6 medium plums, any type, ripe

Roll Pâte Sucrée and use to line a 10-inch tart pan with a removable bottom. Chill ½ hour.

Preheat over to 350°F. Bake empty tart shell 15 minutes. Remove from oven and spread Almond Cream in hot tart shell. Bake another 10 minutes. Remove from oven.

Meanwhile, cut plums in half and remove pits. Arrange plums, cut-side down, over baked Almond Cream; sprinkle with Streusel and bake 20 to 30 minutes, until plums are soft and crust is golden brown. Set aside to cool in pan.

Variations: Use same formula for 10 to 12 ripe apricots—the Streusel is optional. Or fan 5 to 6 ripe pears (thinly sliced lengthwise) over the Almond Cream—no Streusel necessary. For berry tarts, garnish a fully baked Almond Cream tart with about 2½ pints fresh berries.

Walnut Caramel Tart

Don't worry if the quantity of filling seems excessive. It is supposed to form a huge, gooey, sticky dome between two pie shells—definitely not for dieters. We recommend serving it warm with a scoop of vanilla ice cream.

10 to 12 servings

3 cups granulated sugar
1¼ cups water
1½ cups heavy cream
1 cup (2 sticks) unsalted butter
6 cups walnut halves and quarters
1 recipe Pie Dough (page 206)
1 egg, lightly beaten, for glaze

To make filling, combine sugar and water in a large heavy saucepan. Bring to a boil. Cook over moderate heat until caramelized, about 12 minutes. Remove from heat. Gradually add cream, taking care to keep hands clear of the steam that escapes. Stir constantly with a wooden spoon until all lumps dissolve. Break butter into small pieces and add, all at once, to caramel. Whisk until smooth. Stir in walnuts and chill about 2 hours or overnight.

Divide Pie Dough in half. Roll one piece to ⅛-inch thickness and use to line a 9-inch tart pan with a removable bottom, leaving about 1 inch excess all around. Spoon in cooled filling, mounding it high in center. Cover with plastic wrap and set aside in refrigerator.

Roll second piece dough to form a 12-inch circle, ⅛-inch thick. Remove filled shell from refrigerator. Brush egg over overhanging dough. Place rolled dough over filling and carefully seal edges by gently pressing. (It is important to make this a solid seal.) Trim any excess dough with scissors. Flute the edges, using both top and bottom crusts.

Using a paring knife, cut and remove a ¼-inch circle in center of top crust for steam to escape. Brush top with egg and chill 2 to 3 hours, or preferably overnight.

Preheat oven to 350°F. Before baking, brush again with egg and check to make sure top and bottom crusts are sealed together.

Bake 50 minutes to 1 hour or until the edges are golden. Set aside to cool in pan several hours before serving.

Lemon Curd Tarts

Our nut crust is an easy dough to work with. We like the way it offsets the rich lemon custard in these tarts. Ideally, the crust should be as thick as the filling.

8 servings

NUT CRUST

1 cup (2 sticks) unsalted butter, softened

¼ cup granulated sugar

¾ cup finely chopped pecans

1 egg

1 egg yolk

1 teaspoon salt

2¾ cups all-purpose flour

Mix butter, sugar, pecans, whole egg, egg yolk, and salt with a wooden spoon until barely blended. Add flour and knead until a smooth ball forms. Wrap in plastic and chill about 4 hours.

After chilling dough, preheat oven to 350°F. Roll chilled dough to about ¼-inch thickness or divide into 8 parts and press into 8 individual tart pans, 3-inch round × 1-inch deep. The crust should be thick.

Bake empty tart shells 12 to 15 minutes, or until edges begin to brown. Set aside to cool. Meanwhile make Lemon Curd.

LEMON CURD FILLING

1 cup (2 sticks) unsalted butter, melted

2 cups granulated sugar

4 eggs

1 scant cup fresh lemon juice

¾ cup finely chopped pistachio nuts for garnish

Combine butter, sugar, eggs, and lemon juice in a bowl. Place over a pot of simmering water and stir constantly and gently with a spoon or a spatula, being careful not to incorporate air. Continue stirring until mixture is pale yellow and thickly coats the back of a spoon, 7 to 10 minutes. Strain and set aside to cool to room temperature.

Remove cooled tart shells from pans and fill with Lemon Curd. Garnish rims with pistachio nuts and serve.

Variation: For Passion Curd Tarts, substitute 1 cup passion fruit juice for the lemon.

Rhubarb Pie

Mention fruit pies and we automatically think of rhubarb. However, don't hesitate to fill these shells with other fruits of the season. Peaches (peeled, pitted, and cut into wedges) or apples (peeled and diced) mixed with an equal amount of cranberries are delightful.

8 to 10 servings

12 ounces or ⅔ recipe Pie Dough (page 206)
3 pounds rhubarb
1½ to 2 cups granulated sugar to taste
3 tablespoons tapioca
2 cups Streusel (page 201)

Lightly butter a 10-inch pie plate.

On a generously floured board, roll dough to ⅛-inch thickness and line pie plate, leaving about ¼-inch overhang. Pinch up excess dough to form an upright fluted edge. Chill about an hour.

Preheat oven to 350°F. To prebake, line dough with a sheet of parchment paper or aluminum foil and fill with weights, beans, or rice. Bake 25 minutes, remove paper and weights, and set aside. Prepare filling.

Clean rhubarb and cut across width in ½-inch slices. Combine with sugar in a large bowl. Let sit at room temperature 15 minutes. Sprinkle on tapioca, toss well, and let sit an additional 15 minutes.

Pour filling into warm prebaked pie shell and sprinkle Streusel over top. Bake until juices bubble, about 1 hour 15 minutes. Set aside to cool on rack before serving.

Pie Dough

When making Pie Dough, you should be able to see chunks of fat—whether lard, shortening, or butter—in the completed dough. In the oven, they will expand and release the steam that makes pie dough so flaky. All butter may be substituted for the lard, but for the best crust, we still use lard.

makes three 10-inch pie tops or bottoms

3 cups all-purpose flour
¾ cup lard
4 tablespoons (½ stick) unsalted butter
1 teaspoon salt
½ cup plus 2 tablespoons iced water

In a large bowl, combine 2½ cups flour with lard, butter, and salt. Mix lightly with your fingertips until dough forms pea-sized pieces. You should be able to see chunks of fat.

Stir in remaining flour, then stir in water. Lightly knead until dough forms a ball. It is important to handle this dough as little as possible.

Transfer to a plastic bag and form dough into a 6-inch log. Seal bag, pressing out any air, and refrigerate a minimum of 1 hour or as long as 3 days. Pie Dough may be stored in the freezer 1 week.

Divide log in thirds. To roll, soften dough by pressing it in your hands until malleable. Form each into a 4-inch round disk. On a generously floured board, roll from center out, lifting dough, turning it slightly, and occasionally flipping to prevent sticking. Roll dough to ⅛-inch thickness.

Lightly butter and flour a 10-inch pie pan and line with dough, leaving about ¼-inch overhang for shrinkage. Pinch up excess dough to form a rim. Flute edges by pressing the thumb of one hand between the thumb and first finger of the other to form a V pattern. Chill 1 hour.

To bake empty pie shell, preheat oven to 350°F. Line with a sheet of parchment paper or aluminum foil larger than the pan, and fill with pie weights, rice, or beans. Bake about 25 minutes, remove paper and weights, and follow pie recipe directions.

Pâte Sucrée

Our tart pastry is sweet and rich, almost like cookie dough. If you are just learning to bake, this is a good, easy dough to start with. Excellent for fruit tarts as well as rolled sugar cookies.

makes two 9- or 10-inch tart shells plus a few cookies

8 tablespoons (1 stick) unsalted butter, softened
1 cup plus 6 tablespoons confectioners' sugar, sifted
1 egg
1 teaspoon salt
1¾ cups all-purpose flour

In an electric mixer, cream together butter and sugar until light and fluffy. Add egg and salt, and beat until combined. Add flour, all at once, and slowly mix just until flour is evenly moistened. You don't want to mix until a ball forms around beaters.

Transfer to a plastic bag and form dough into a 6-inch log. Seal bag, pressing out any air, and refrigerate a minimum of 4 hours or as long as 4 days. (Well-wrapped Pâte Sucrée may be stored in the freezer a month.)

Divide log in half for one tart shell. To roll, soften dough by pressing it in your hands until malleable. Form a 4-inch round disk. On a lightly floured board, roll from center out, lifting dough, turning it slightly, and occasionally flipping to prevent sticking. Flour board as necessary. Roll dough to ⅛-inch thickness.

To line a tart pan, fold dough in half and lift. Place in pan, unfold, and gently press it evenly into bottom and up sides of pan. Create a lip at top by pressing dough between flutes of pan with your fingers as you pinch dough off at the edge. Then for an even crust, roll a rolling pin across top. Dough scraps can be used to patch short edges or holes, or for cookies. Chill ½ hour before baking.

To bake empty tart shell, preheat oven to 350°F. Bake 20 minutes for a fully baked shell or 15 minutes for a partially baked.

Baked Custards

Indian Pudding

Fresh squeezed ginger juice gives this homey American dessert additional zing. We love to serve it piping hot with a spoonful or two of cold cream or a scoop of vanilla ice cream.

8 servings

2 cups milk
½ cup yellow cornmeal
¼ cup granulated sugar
¼ cup packed brown sugar
½ cup molasses
1 teaspoon salt
2 tablespoons unsalted butter
¼ teaspoon ground cloves
3 cups half and half
1 3-inch piece of fresh ginger

Preheat oven to 325°F. Butter a 9 × 5 × 3-inch Pyrex loaf pan.

Combine milk and cornmeal in a medium stainless or enamel saucepan. Cook over moderate heat, whisking constantly, until mixture comes to a boil. Reduce heat to low and continue stirring until as thick as oatmeal. Remove from heat.

Add the granulated sugar, brown sugar, molasses, salt, butter, and cloves and 2 cups half and half. Stir to combine. Bring mixture back to a boil and transfer to prepared loaf pan.

Place inside a larger pan and pour in boiling water until it rises halfway up the sides of the loaf pan. Bake 1 hour, stirring after the first ½ hour.

Peel and grate ginger. Press against a fine sieve or squeeze through a piece of cheesecloth to extract a tablespoon or two of juice.

After baking an hour, add ginger juice and remaining cup of half and half, and stir. Bake an additional hour, stirring each ½ hour. Serve immediately in small bowls or cups, or store in refrigerator and reheat over low heat.

Crème Caramel

One of the great rewards of cooking is making a perfect, velvety Crème Caramel—and then tasting it. The quintessential summer dessert, this delightfully simple dish can be prepared in advance.

8 to 10 servings

CARAMEL

2 cups granulated sugar

1¼ cups water

CUSTARD

8 eggs

4 egg yolks

1 cup plus 2 tablespoons granulated sugar

1 quart half and half

½ cup Triple Sec or Grand Marnier

2 teaspoons vanilla extract

Preheat oven to 325°F.

For caramel, combine sugar and ½ cup water in a medium saucepan. Be sure all sugar granules are washed down from pot sides. Cook over moderate heat, swirling pan occasionally, until color is golden brown and mixture smells like caramel. Often you need to cook it a bit darker than you would imagine. This should take 10 to 15 minutes. Pour enough caramel into a 9-inch round cake pan to coat bottom and sides. Swirl to coat and reserve.

Add remaining water to caramel in saucepan. Bring to a boil and cook over moderate heat until the sugar dissolves, about 5 minutes. Occasionally stir and brush down sides with a pastry brush dipped in cold water. This process prevents crystallization of the sugar. Set this caramel sauce aside at room temperature, then chill until serving time.

Combine all custard ingredients in a large bowl. Gently whisk together, being careful not to incorporate much air.

Strain half custard into prepared cake pan. Place inside a larger pan and pour in boiling water until it rises halfway up the sides of the cake pan. Set the roasting pan on the open oven door and strain in remaining custard.

(continued)

Bake for 1 hour to 1 hour 15 minutes, until center feels just firm when pressed. Set aside to cool about 1½ hours. Cover with plastic wrap touching top. Refrigerate overnight or as long as 4 days.

To serve, run a knife along inside edge, 2 or 3 times, to loosen. When you press center, sides should pull away. Cover with a platter and quickly invert. Carefully drain excess caramel into a bowl and strain into reserved cold sauce. Serve wedges of Crème Caramel on dessert plates. Top with chilled caramel sauce.

Bread Pudding with Raspberry Sauce

The difference between good and great bread pudding lies in the standing time. It should be long enough for the bread to absorb the liquids before baking. Bread pudding is delicious hot or cold.

10 servings

6 eggs
¾ cup granulated sugar
4 cups half and half
¼ cup Triple Sec or Grand Marnier
2 teaspoons vanilla extract
grated zest of 1 orange
6 cups dry white bread, crusts removed, and cut into ½-inch dice
2 tablespoons unsalted butter, softened
1 tablespoon granulated sugar plus 1 teaspoon cinnamon for sprinkling
1 pint fresh raspberries
Raspberry Sauce, recipe follows

Generously butter a 9 × 5 × 3-inch Pyrex loaf pan.

In a large bowl, whisk together eggs and sugar. Add half and half, Triple Sec, vanilla, and orange zest, and mix until combined. Add bread cubes and toss until the bread is evenly moistened. Transfer to prepared loaf pan and let stand at room temperature at least ½ hour, preferably 1 hour.

Preheat oven to 325°F.

Dot bread pudding with softened butter. Sprinkle on sugar and cinnamon. Place inside a larger pan and pour in warm water until it rises halfway up the sides of the loaf pan.

Bake 1 hour 15 minutes to 1 hour 30 minutes, until top is brown and crusty.

To serve hot, scoop and serve individual portions in bowls, topped with fresh berries. Or, chill 4 to 6 hours, invert onto a serving platter, and serve ½-inch slices with Raspberry Sauce.

Raspberry Sauce

1 cup granulated sugar
1 cup water
1 pint basket fresh or frozen raspberries

Combine sugar and water in a small saucepan and boil about 1 minute. Add raspberries, return to a boil, and cook, whisking constantly until the berries are smooth, about 3 minutes. Pass through a fine sieve and chill until serving time.

makes 1½ cups

Sweet Potato Flan

*This is one of our most
popular winter desserts.
Why bother with a crust
when you have a
custard this dense and
satisfying? For a
pumpkin flan,
substitute 2 cups of
pureed pumpkin.*

10 servings

2 pounds sweet potatoes

CARAMEL

2 cups granulated sugar

1¼ cups water

CUSTARD

1⅓ cups packed brown sugar

8 eggs

2 cups heavy cream

3 tablespoons brandy

2 teaspoons vanilla extract

1 tablespoon freshly grated ginger (page 235)

1 teaspoon salt

½ teaspoon cinnamon

¼ teaspoon ground cloves

¼ teaspoon ground allspice

Preheat oven to 350°F. Bake potatoes until soft throughout, about 1 hour. Cool, then peel and cut into chunks. Puree in a food processor—do not overmix—and reserve. Reduce oven to 325°F.

Prepare caramel and sauce following the same method as for Crème Caramel (page 209). Line a 3-quart Pyrex loaf pan with caramel and set aside on a level surface. Chill sauce.

Combine custard ingredients in a large bowl and whisk to combine. Pour through a strainer into lined loaf pan.

Place inside a larger roasting pan. Pour in boiling water until it rises halfway up the sides of the loaf pan. Bake about 1 hour 50 minutes. The center should feel firm when pressed.

Set aside to cool about 1½ hours. Cover with plastic wrap touching top. Refrigerate overnight or as long as 4 days.

Run a knife along inside edge 2 or 3 times to loosen. When you press center, sides should pull away. Cover with a platter and quickly invert. Drain excess caramel into a bowl and strain into reserved cold sauce. Serve slices of flan on dessert plates. Top with chilled caramel sauce.

Cheesecake

We eliminated the crust in our otherwise classic cheesecake so that people could get right to the cheese. Serve it plain or with the fruit toppings suggested here.

8 to 10 servings

½ cup sliced almonds, toasted
2½ pounds cream cheese, softened
1 cup plus 2 tablespoons granulated sugar
1½ teaspoons grated lemon zest
⅓ cup fresh lemon juice
3 eggs
1½ teaspoons vanilla extract

Preheat oven to 325°F. Butter a 9-inch round cake pan and line bottom and sides with almonds.

With an electric mixer at low speed, beat cream cheese until soft and smooth. With machine running, add sugar, lemon zest, and juice, beating well between additions. Add eggs, one at a time, beating well after each addition. Beat in vanilla. To ensure even mixing, be sure to scrape down bowl between additions.

Pour batter into lined cake pan. Tap it 3 or 4 times on the counter to eliminate air pockets. Place inside a larger pan and pour in boiling water until it rises halfway up the sides of the cake pan. Bake about 45 minutes, until center feels firm when pressed.

Set aside to cool on rack, then refrigerate 2 or 3 hours. To unmold, place pan over a low burner about 2 minutes. Invert onto a platter, then invert again—the nuts should be on the bottom. The completed cake may be kept in refrigerator up to 3 days.

Variations: To cut sweetness and add color, garnish with fresh berries—2 baskets of strawberries or blueberries. Brush with a glaze made from ¼ cup apricot jelly heated with 3 tablespoons water.

Cookies and Cakes

Chewy Date Bars

These great old-fashioned sandwich bars are crunchy on the top and bottom, and chewy inside. Use them to stuff lunch boxes, serve with a bowl of vanilla ice cream for dessert, or cut into small squares for afternoon tea.

makes 12 large squares

1 pound pitted dried dates, chopped
1 cup water
1 cup granulated sugar
½ cup fresh lemon juice
3 cups rolled oats
2½ cups all-purpose flour
1¾ cups packed brown sugar
¾ teaspoon baking soda
¾ teaspoon salt
1¾ cups (3½ sticks) unsalted butter, melted

Preheat oven to 350°F. Generously butter a 9 × 12-inch pan.

Combine dates and water in a saucepan. Cook at a low boil for 5 minutes, until mixture is as thick as mashed potatoes. Stir in sugar and remove from heat. Add lemon juice and set aside to cool.

In a large bowl, mix together oats, flour, brown sugar, baking soda, and salt. Add melted butter to dry mixture. Stir to evenly moisten.

Spread half oat mixture in baking pan to form an even layer. Cover evenly with all date mixture. Spread remaining oat mixture over top.

Bake about 40 minutes, until top is golden brown and pebbly. The edges should start caramelizing. Set aside to cool, in pan on rack, about 1 hour. Run a sharp knife along inside edges to loosen. Invert, trim edges, and cut into squares.

Brownies

These traditional brownies are great for taking along on picnics. They don't crumble or crack and everybody loves them.

makes 12 large or 20 small brownies

5 ounces unsweetened bitter chocolate, chopped
1¼ cups (2½ sticks) unsalted butter
½ teaspoon salt
2½ cups granulated sugar
5 eggs
1 teaspoon vanilla extract
1¼ cups all-purpose flour
2½ cups walnuts, roughly chopped

Preheat oven to 325°F. Butter and flour a 9 × 12-inch pan and line with parchment paper.

Combine chocolate, butter, and salt in the top of a double boiler or in a bowl. Melt over simmering water and set aside to cool.

In a large bowl, combine sugar, eggs, and vanilla. Whisk until smooth. Add melted chocolate mixture and whisk to combine.

Fold in flour until it just disappears. Fold in walnuts. Spread batter evenly in pan.

Bake for about 35 minutes or until a toothpick inserted in center comes out clean. Set aside to cool, in pan on rack, 1 hour. Invert pan to release and cut into squares.

Gâteau St.-Honoré

Make sure you have a good night's sleep before tackling this one. Of the many parts in this spectacular cake, the puff pastry, Pastry Cream, and City Chocolate can all be made a day or more in advance. But allow plenty of time for the assembly.

This cake is definitely a challenge even for experienced bakers, but for a truly special occasion, well worth the effort.

10 servings

1 pound puff pastry

CREAM PUFFS

½ cup milk

3½ tablespoons unsalted butter

⅛ teaspoon salt

½ cup plus 1 tablespoon all-purpose flour

2 eggs

Pastry Cream, recipe follows

1½ cups sugar for caramel

½ cup water

½ recipe City Chocolate (page 194), omitting the Espresso Crème Anglaise

2 cups heavy cream, cold

3 ounces semisweet chocolate, melted

Roll puff pastry to form a 10-inch square and reserve in the refrigerator.

To make Cream Puffs, combine milk, butter, and salt in a medium-heavy saucepan. Bring to a boil. Add flour all at once. Mix quickly with a wooden spoon until a ball forms on the spoon and the flour is evenly moistened. Transfer to a bowl and add eggs, one at a time, beating well after each addition.

Preheat oven to 450°F.

Fill a pastry bag fitted with a large plain tip with dough and line a baking sheet with parchment paper. Pipe dough onto baking sheet to form small circles, about the size of quarters. With a finger dipped in cold water, flatten point on top of each puff. Drop pan on the counter to set puffs.

Bake until uniformly puffed and golden, about 10 minutes. Reduce heat to 375°F and bake an additional 15 to 20 minutes. You can test for doneness by opening a puff. The inside should be totally dry. Set aside to cool on a rack.

Turn heat up to 425°F. Place puff pastry on a parchment paper–lined baking sheet and, with a 10-inch round cake pan inverted over dough, trace a 10-inch circle using a sharp knife. This will be the base for the cake. Prick all over with a fork and set in refrigerator to rest 15 minutes. Then bake for 20 minutes, until puffed and golden. Reserve at room temperature.

Meanwhile make Pastry Cream. Fill a pastry bag fitted with a #2 tip with the cream. Make a hole in bottom of each puff using a small paring knife. Fill with Pastry Cream and reserve.

Combine sugar and water for caramelizing in a saucepan and cook until golden brown. Follow the method used for Crème Caramel (page 209). Immediately remove from heat. Using a fork, dip half of each cream puff into warm caramel and place on a tray lined with parchment paper. When caramel has set, turn puff and dip uncoated half in caramel. Immediately arrange puffs, flat-side up, along edge of cooled puff pastry to form an even wall.

Fill center of pastry with an even layer of City Chocolate. Whip cold cream until soft peaks form. Fold half of this cream into melted chocolate and set aside.

Spoon remaining whipped cream into a pastry bag fitted with a #8 plain tip. Pipe about 5 rows of Hershey's Kiss–shaped domes over chocolate filling, leaving even spaces between rows. Fill bag with chocolate-flavored cream and repeat, filling spaces between rows. Chill until serving time.

(continued)

PASTRY CREAM

½ cup granulated sugar
¼ cup cornstarch
4 egg yolks
2 cups milk
½ teaspoon vanilla

Mix ¼ cup sugar and all cornstarch in a bowl until smooth. Add egg yolks and mix until a paste is formed. Stir in ½ cup milk.

Combine remaining milk and sugar in a saucepan and bring to a boil. Pour hot mixture into mixture in bowl, whisking constantly. Pour back into pan.

Cook over moderate heat, stirring constantly, until smooth and thick. Remove from heat and stir an additional minute. Stir in vanilla and transfer to a bowl. Cover with buttered parchment paper touching top and chill a minimum of 2 hours or as long as 2 days.

makes 2½ cups

Desserts and Beverages

Poppy Seed Cake with Lemon Glaze

This is a classic dessert cake, but at home, nothing beats a toasted slice with morning coffee. The best coffee cake ever—guaranteed.

8 to 10 servings

1 cup poppy seeds

⅓ cup honey

¼ cup water

12 tablespoons (1½ sticks) unsalted butter, softened

¾ cup granulated sugar

1 tablespoon grated lemon zest

1 teaspoon vanilla extract

2 eggs

2¼ cups all-purpose flour

1 teaspoon baking soda

1 teaspoon baking powder

1 teaspoon salt

2½ tablespoons fresh lemon juice

1 cup sour cream

Lemon Glaze, recipe follows

Preheat oven to 325°F. Butter and flour a 10-inch tube pan.

Combine poppy seeds, honey, and water in a medium saucepan. Cook over moderate heat, stirring frequently, until water evaporates and mixture looks like wet sand. This will take about 5 minutes. Set aside to cool.

Cream together butter and sugar until light and fluffy. Mix in lemon zest and vanilla. Add eggs, one at a time, beating well after each addition.

In another bowl, combine flour, baking soda, baking powder, and salt.

When poppy seed mixture has cooled, stir in lemon juice. Pour into creamed butter mixture and stir until combined.

By hand, add dry ingredients and sour cream in three stages, alternating liquid and dry, and ending with sour cream. Spoon batter into prepared pan, smoothing top with a spatula, and tap vigorously on a counter to eliminate air pockets.

Bake about 1 hour 15 minutes, until a toothpick inserted in center comes out clean. Set aside to cool, in pan on rack, about 15 minutes. Invert onto platter and prepare Lemon Glaze.

Brush hot Lemon Glaze all over bottom, top, and sides of cake to flavor it and seal in moisture.

Lemon Glaze

> 1 cup granulated sugar
> ½ cup fresh lemon juice

makes 1¼ cups

Combine sugar and lemon juice in a small saucepan. Bring to a boil over moderate heat and cook a minute or two, until sugar is dissolved. Remove from heat.

Shortbreads

Shortbreads are quick and easy—nice to have on hand for afternoon coffee or tea.

10 servings

1 cup (2 sticks) unsalted butter, softened
⅓ cup packed brown sugar
¼ cup granulated sugar
1 cup all-purpose flour
1 cup pastry flour
¼ cup cornstarch
¾ teaspoon salt
⅓ cup pecan halves

Preheat oven to 325°F. Have ready an ungreased 10-inch tart pan with a removable bottom.

Cream together the butter, brown sugar, and granulated sugar until light and fluffy.

In another bowl, mix together the all-purpose flour, pastry flour, cornstarch, and salt. Add dry ingredients to creamed mixture and stir until combined.

With your fingers, spread dough evenly over pan, like a thick pie crust. (Occasionally dip your fingers into flour, if the dough is too sticky.) When you have an even layer, flute edges by pressing your fingers around rim to form 1-inch long ridges. Arrange pecans, flat-side down, in a circular pattern, in spaces between ridges. If you wish, you can decorate by pressing the tines of a fork into dough to form a pattern. Prick all over with a fork.

Bake until golden and slightly puffy, about 45 minutes. Set aside to cool on rack. Cut in wedges to serve.

Gâteau Benoît

We like to top this simple, light cake with a generous pile of chocolate shavings, but feel free to simplify the presentation. This exceptionally moist cake is just as delicious with a sprinkling of confectioners' sugar or a dollop of whipped cream.

8 servings

7½ ounces semisweet chocolate, chopped
11 tablespoons (1 stick plus 3 tablespoons) unsalted butter
4 eggs, separated
½ cup plus 1 tablespoon granulated sugar
½ cup all-purpose flour

Preheat oven to 350°F. Butter and flour a 10-inch round cake pan. Line with parchment paper.

Melt chocolate and butter together in the top of a double boiler or in a bowl over simmering water. Set aside to cool.

Beat egg yolks until light and fluffy, then slowly add sugar, beating constantly until pale yellow. Fold in melted chocolate mixture.

Sift flour over chocolate mixture and mix until flour just disappears.

Whisk egg whites until soft peaks form. Fold whites into chocolate mixture in two parts. Pour batter into pan, spread evenly, and tap once or twice on a counter to remove air.

Bake 20 to 25 minutes, until a toothpick inserted in center comes out with a few flakes clinging to it. Set aside to cool, in pan on rack, about an hour.

To release cake, run a knife along inside edge to loosen. Invert onto serving platter, peel off parchment, and invert again. Prepare chocolate curls.

Pile curls on top of cake in a circular pattern pointing outward from the center. Dust with confectioners' sugar.

CHOCOLATE CURLS

1-pound or larger block semisweet chocolate
confectioners' sugar for dusting

The key to making chocolate curls, or cigarettes, is the right temperature. Place chocolate in oven, with only the pilot light on, 10 to 20 minutes, until it softens slightly. Or place in an oven that's off but still warm until chocolate *just* begins to soften. In warm weather, this step may not be necessary.

Then, holding the handle of a heavy chef's knife with both hands and applying even pressure, pull blade across surface of block, toward you, at about a 60° angle. With some practice you can make either tight cigarette rolls or freeform ruffles. Leftover chocolate can be wrapped in plastic and used again.

Chocolate Chip Cookies

At home we like to keep a log of this rich dough in the refrigerator for midnight cravings. You can cut 1-inch slices and bake small quantities as the occasion demands.

makes 40 small or 14 jumbo cookies

1 cup (2 sticks) unsalted butter, softened
¾ cup granulated sugar
¾ cup light brown sugar
1 teaspoon vanilla extract
2 eggs
2½ cups all-purpose flour
1 teaspoon baking soda
1 teaspoon salt
6 ounces semisweet chocolate, chopped, or chocolate chips

Preheat oven to 350°F. Lightly butter and flour a cookie sheet or line with parchment paper.

Cream butter. Gradually add granulated and light brown sugars, continuing to cream until there are no lumps and the mixture is light and fluffy. Stir in vanilla. Add eggs, one at a time, beating well after each addition.

Mix flour, baking soda, and salt in another bowl. Add, all at once, to butter mixture and mix until combined. Fold in chocolate. Dough may be stored in the refrigerator wrapped in plastic 5 days.

Spoon about 1 tablespoon batter each for small cookies and 3 tablespoons each for jumbos onto prepared cookie sheets. Bake about 15 minutes for small—20 minutes for jumbos. The edges should just begin to turn golden. Set aside to cool on racks.

Old-Fashioned Peanut Butter Cookies

These childhood favorites are great for filling lunch boxes and cookie jars.

makes 40 small or 12 jumbo cookies

1 cup (2 sticks) unsalted butter, softened
¾ cup granulated sugar
1 cup packed brown sugar
1 cup soft peanut butter, smooth or crunchy
2 eggs
1 teaspoon vanilla extract
2 cups all-purpose flour
1 teaspoon salt
1 teaspoon baking soda

Preheat oven to 350°F. Lightly butter and flour a cookie sheet or line with parchment paper.

Cream together butter, granulated sugar and brown sugar. Stir in peanut butter until smooth. Add eggs and vanilla. Mix until well combined.

In another bowl, mix together flour, salt, and baking soda. Add to peanut butter mixture and stir just until flour disappears.

Spoon about 1 tablespoon batter each for small cookies and 3 tablespoons each for jumbos onto prepared cookie sheets. Dip the tines of a fork into flour and score each cookie in a traditional crisscross pattern. Bake about 15 minutes for small cookies and 20 minutes for jumbos. The edges should just begin to turn golden. Set aside to cool on racks.

Oatmeal Rum Raisin Cookies

Rum-plumped raisins add an adult twist to another childhood favorite. We don't think kids will mind the change.

makes 50 small or 18 jumbo cookies

¾ cup raisins

¼ cup rum

12 tablespoons (1½ sticks) unsalted butter, softened

1½ cups packed brown sugar

½ cup granulated sugar

2 tablespoons molasses

2 eggs

¼ cup milk

1 cup grated, unsweetened coconut

2 cups rolled oats

2½ cups all-purpose flour

½ teaspoon baking powder

½ teaspoon salt

Preheat oven to 350°F. Lightly butter and flour a cookie sheet or line with parchment.

Combine raisins and rum in a small saucepan. Heat over low flame until most liquid has been absorbed. Set aside to cool.

Cream butter, brown sugar, granulated sugar, and molasses until light and fluffy. Add eggs, one at a time, beating well after each addition. Stir in milk.

In another bowl, mix together coconut, oats, flour, baking powder, and salt. Set aside.

Add raisins and rum to creamed mixture and briefly stir. Add dry ingredients and stir until well combined.

Spoon about 1 tablespoon batter each for small cookies and 3 tablespoons each for jumbos onto prepared cookie sheet. Bake about 15 minutes for small and 25 minutes for jumbos. The edges should just begin to turn golden. Set aside to cool on racks.

Ice Cream Shells

It takes some practice to get the knack of molding these thin, crisp cookies. They make a delightful, light dessert filled with homemade ice cream, such as the Lemon Ice Cream on page 228, and fruit.

makes 12 cookie
shells

1 tablespoon soft butter and 1 tablespoon flour for coating pan
2 egg whites
¼ cup milk
1 teaspoon vanilla extract
⅛ teaspoon salt
4 tablespoons (½ stick) unsalted butter, melted
1 cup confectioners' sugar, sifted
¾ cup all-purpose flour, sifted
¾ cup sliced almonds

Preheat oven to 400°F. Combine the tablespoon each butter and flour to make a paste. Spread over a cookie sheet and set aside.

Combine egg whites, milk, vanilla, and salt in a bowl and let sit until room temperature. (You can speed the process by slightly warming mixture over a pan of hot water.)

Add melted butter. Whisk in sugar until evenly blended. Add flour and whisk until smooth.

Allowing about 6 inches for spreading, spoon 1½ tablespoons batter for each cookie onto prepared cookie sheet. With a spatula, spread batter to form a thin 5-inch circle, leaving about an inch between cookies.

Scatter some almonds over batter.

Bake about 3 to 5 minutes, until lightly golden all over. Immediately place each cookie over an inverted coffee cup or custard cup. Cover with a dry cloth and press down to mold. Cookies will stiffen in 1 to 2 minutes. Continue until all cookies are baked. Serve immediately or store in airtight tins. A cookie sheet will hold about 3 cookies per batch. Coat the cooled sheet with butter and flour paste each time.

Lemon Ice Cream

makes 1½ quarts

7 lemons, washed
1½ cups heavy cream
2 cups half and half
9 egg yolks
1 cup granulated sugar
2 teaspoons vanilla extract

Grate zest of all lemons, taking care to get only the yellow part—no white. Squeeze juice from 4 lemons and reserve.

Combine cream, half and half, and lemon zest in a medium-heavy saucepan. Bring to a boil.

In a large bowl, whisk together egg yolks and sugar until thick and pale yellow. Pour in boiling liquid and stir until combined. Stir in lemon juice and vanilla. Strain into a large container and refrigerate until cold, or place in a bowl nested in a larger bowl of iced water and stir occasionally until cold.

Pour into your ice cream maker and follow manufacturer's instructions. Store in freezer 1 to 2 days.

Beverages

Lemon Ginger Tea

This spicy iced tea is the very best thirst quencher. Served hot with cinnamon sticks, it is great when you aren't feeling well.

makes 1 quart

1 quart water
juice of 1 lemon
¼ cup freshly grated ginger (page 235)
¼ cup honey
thin slices of lemon and lime for garnish

Bring water to a boil. Add lemon juice, the squeezed lemon, and ginger. Let steep about 20 minutes. Stir in honey. Line a strainer with a thin wet cloth and strain tea into a pitcher. Chill thoroughly and serve on ice with thin slices of lemon and lime.

Yogi Tea

makes 2 quarts

2 quarts water
¼ cup milk
¼ cup half and half
⅓ cup granulated sugar
2 cinnamon sticks
1 teaspoon freshly grated ginger (page 235)
2 teaspoons whole cloves
2 teaspoons cardamom seeds
½ teaspoon freshly ground black pepper

Bring water to a boil, then reduce to a simmer. Add milk, half and half, sugar, and cinnamon, and simmer for 15 minutes. Add remaining ingredients and simmer an additional 30 minutes. Strain and serve hot or cold.

City Herb Cooler

This cool, red drink is especially pretty garnished with thin slices of lime. Hibiscus flowers or rose hips, great sources of vitamin C, are available in Mexican and American markets.

makes 1 quart

1 quart water
¾ cup dried hibiscus flowers or rose hips
¼ cup honey
thin slices of lime for garnish (optional)

Bring water to a boil. Add hibiscus flowers and let steep 15 minutes. Stir in honey. Line a strainer with a thin wet cloth and strain tea into a pitcher. Serve immediately, or chill and serve over ice with thin slices of lime.

Iced Mocha

Iced Mocha is thick like a milk shake but without the ice cream.

makes 1 glass

1 tablespoon chocolate syrup
1 cup double espresso or very strong coffee, hot
¼ cup half and half
4 ice cubes

Stir chocolate syrup into hot coffee until melted.
Transfer to a blender, add half and half and ice cubes, and blend at high speed for 2 to 3 minutes. Serve immediately in a tall, cold glass.

Indian Iced Tea

makes 1 quart

2 cups half and half
2 cups water
2 tablespoons black Indian tea leaves, such as Ceylon
6 tablespoons granulated sugar

Bring half and half and water to a boil. Add tea and simmer for 15 minutes. Stir in sugar, strain, and chill. Serve over ice in a tall glass.

Egg Nog

Homemade Egg Nog is a cinch to make. Mix it at least 6 hours in advance to mellow the tastes and add rum or brandy as the occasion demands.

makes 1 quart

6 eggs
1 cup confectioners' sugar
3 cups half and half or milk
2 tablespoons vanilla extract
¼ teaspoon salt
freshly grated nutmeg to taste

In an electric mixer, set at high speed, beat eggs and sugar until light. Reduce speed to low. Add half and half, vanilla, and salt, and continue beating until thoroughly combined. Chill 6 to 8 hours. Serve garnished with nutmeg.

Glossary of Ingredients and Techniques

Ingredients

Ancho Chile is a rich, mild-flavored dried poblano chile. It is medium-sized, with a triangular shape, deep mahogany color, and pebbly texture. Available in Mexican markets and some supermarkets.

Basmati is an aromatic, long-grained white rice grown at the base of the Himalaya mountains. It is distinguished by a small hook at one end and a nutty flavor. Available in Indian and health food markets and gourmet shops.

Black Fungus or Wood Ear Mushrooms are a rubbery, slightly crunchy fungus used to add color and texture in Thai and Chinese cuisines. Available in dehydrated form in Asian markets and some supermarkets.

Black Mustard Seeds are the tiny, reddish brown seeds of the black mustard plant. Used in Indian cuisine, they are available in Indian or Middle Eastern markets. Yellow mustard seeds may be substituted.

Brown Rice Vinegar is a Japanese vinegar made from fermented brown rice. Available in Japanese and health food markets. Rice wine vinegar may be substituted.

Bulgarian Feta is a salty goat cheese, stored in brine. It is creamier and milder than the Greek variety. Available in good cheese shops and Armenian markets.

Bulgur Wheat is a coarse cracked wheat that has been cooked. It always needs to be reconstituted. Available in Middle Eastern and health food markets in a variety of grinds.

Cellophane Noodles or Bean Threads are thin translucent Chinese noodles made from ground mung beans. Available in the Asian section of most supermarkets.

Chick-pea Flour is a fine, powdery flour made from milled, dried garbanzo beans. Available in Indian, Middle Eastern, and health food markets.

Chili Paste is a bottled sauce of red chiles, garlic, and salt. Available in Asian markets and supermarkets.

Chinese Sausage (Lop Cheung) is a very firm, slightly bumpy pork sausage with a sweet smoky flavor. Available in Asian markets.

Coconut Milk (unsweetened) is a Thai product made by grinding fresh coconut with water. It is available in cans in Asian markets and in some supermarkets.

Daikon Spiced Sprouts are sprouted Japanese daikon radish seeds. Available in Japanese markets and fine produce markets.

Dal is the Indian name for the inside of any whole, dried bean. Urid dal, black bean dal, and orange dal are three varieties available in Indian or Middle Eastern markets. Lentils may be substituted.

Dried Shrimp are tiny, shelled, salty shrimp used as a spice. Available in Asian and Mexican markets.

Garam Masala is a blend of Indian dried spices which varies, like a curry, according to taste. Usually contains a combination of finely ground black pepper, cumin, coriander, and cardamom. Available in Indian and some health food markets or try making your own with ground spices.

Geoduck Clams are huge, long-necked clams from the Pacific Northwest. They are usually ground and used in chowders. Available in Asian fish markets.

Hoisin Sauce is a thick, soybean-based, sweet Chinese sauce usually mixed with other condiments for marinades and sauces. Available in bottles or cans in Asian markets and supermarkets.

Kaffir Lime Leaves are the dried leaves of the Thai kaffir lime tree. These brittle, bitter leaves are available in Thai markets or by mail order.

Kirbies or Pickling Cucumbers are small, pale green cucumbers with fewer seeds and a milder flavor than larger cucumbers. Available in supermarkets.

Mirin is a sweet Japanese cooking wine made with rice wine (sake) and sugar. Available in Japanese markets and the Asian section of supermarkets.

Oyster Sauce is a thick, salty Chinese sauce made from oyster extract, soy sauce, and sugar. It is available in bottles in Asian markets and supermarkets.

Palm or Coconut Sugar is a very sweet, hard-packed brown sugar made from the coconut palm tree. Imported from Thailand, it is available in cans in Asian markets. Brown sugar may be substituted.

Plum Sauce is a sweet and sour Chinese sauce made from plums, vinegar, sugar, ginger, and garlic. It is available in bottles in Asian markets and supermarkets.

Rice Sticks are dried, white Chinese vermicelli made from rice and water. They can be boiled in water until translucent and soft, or deep fried in oil until puffy and crisp. Available in Asian markets and supermarkets.

Rice Wine Vinegar is a full-flavored, yellow Japanese vinegar made from rice wine. Available in Asian markets and supermarkets.

San Bai Su is a Japanese seasoning sauce made from equal parts mirin, soy sauce, and brown rice vinegar. Available in bottles at Japanese markets or mix your own.

Soba Noodles are thin, dark Japanese noodles made from buckwheat flour. Available in Japanese and health food markets.

Tahini is a paste made from ground sesame seeds. Available in Middle Eastern markets and supermarkets.

Tamarind is a brittle, brown seed pod that grows on trees. When the dried pod is peeled, soaked, and strained it produces a thick paste with a unique sweet and tart flavor. The paste is used in chutneys, soft drinks, and meat sauces. Available in Mexican markets and some supermarkets.

Thai Fish Sauce or Nam Pla is a salty brown sauce, similar to soy sauce, made of anchovy, fish or shrimp extract and salt. Available in Asian markets and supermarkets.

Thai Red Curry Paste is a hot paste of ground red chiles, onion, garlic, lemon grass, lime peel, and shrimp paste. It is available in Thai markets and by mail order.

Techniques

Clarified butter has a higher burning point than ordinary butter because the milk solids are removed. To separate the solids, melt butter in heavy saucepan over moderate heat. Simmer until the butter foams, then skim and discard the white froth that forms at the top. Carefully pour the remaining butter through a cheesecloth, allowing the white sediment to remain at the bottom of the pan. By clarifying, the volume is reduced by one quarter.

To crack peppercorns, place the whole peppercorns on a work counter. Place the bottom of a heavy skillet or saucepan on top and push down and away from you.

To debeard mussels, pinch the hairlike beard and slide up and down until it releases.

To grate fresh ginger in quantity, first peel the root, then cut into thin slices. With the machine running, drop through the feed tube of a food processor fitted with metal blade. Combine with a small amount of rice wine vinegar and store in the refrigerator as long as 2 weeks.

To make bread crumbs, first dry the bread (French or Italian loaves, with crust, are good) in a 300°F oven for 20 to 30 minutes. Cut into chunks and blend in a food processor until fine. Sift through a fine sieve and store in a cool, dry place.

To peel and seed tomatoes, remove the cores and score an X on the underside. Blanch for 15 seconds in boiling water and immediately plunge into iced water to prevent cooking. Peel with a paring knife. Cut in half across the width and squeeze to remove the seeds or scoop them out with a spoon.

To puree garlic in quantity, break the bulbs apart and peel, first by flattening the cloves with the flat side of a heavy knife or cleaver, then removing the skin. Puree with a small amount of olive oil, in a food processor fitted with a metal blade or in a blender. Store in the refrigerator as long as 2 weeks.

To render fat, boil at a slow simmer until the solids settle to the bottom and water evaporates. The remaining clear liquid can be stored in the refrigerator and used for sautéeing.

To roast peppers, place on a baking sheet under a preheated broiler and cook, turning occasionally, until the peppers are evenly charred. Transfer to a plastic bag, tie a knot at the top, and set aside to steam about 10 minutes. Peel under cold, running water.

To roast seeds (like mustard), cook in a dry sauté pan over medium-low heat, shaking occasionally, until the seeds smoke slightly and release their aroma. Or place on a baking sheet in a 250°F oven for 10 to 15 minutes, shaking the pan occasionally.

To toast and skin nuts, spread the nuts on a sheet pan and cook for 10 to 15 minutes in a 350°F oven, shaking occasionally. Wrap in a clean, damp towel for 10 minutes. Remove the towel and rub the nuts between your hands to remove the husks.

Index

Horseradish (*continued*)
 mustard-marinated skirt steak
  with, 75
Hot brisket of beef sandwiches, 63
House dressing, limestone lettuce
 with, 164

I

Ice cream:
 lemon, 228
 shells, 227
Iced mocha, 230
Indian iced tea, 231
Indian pudding, 208
Ingredients, 232–235

K

Kaffir lime leaves, 234
Kidneys, veal, with lemon and soy,
 89
Kirbies (pickling cucumbers), 234

L

Lamb:
 curry with fried onions, 85–86
 herb-stuffed leg of, with pimento
  sauce, 79–80
 moussaka, 81–83
 with sautéed eggplant and onion
  marmalade on naan, 61
 shanks, braised, with oregano and
  feta, 84
 or veal stock, brown, 57–58
Lamb's tongue with thyme
 vinaigrette, 18
Leeks:
 with caraway, 171
 coulis of, roasted halibut with,
  114–115
Lemon:
 butter, turkey breast with, 100
 curd tarts, 204–205
 ginger tea, 229
 glaze, 220

hazelnut tart, 198–199
ice cream, 228
veal kidneys with soy and, 89
Lentil(s):
 orange dal with ginger and garlic,
  136
 soup, 39
 and walnut salad, 134
Lettuce:
 cream of, soup, 36
 limestone, with house dressing,
  164
Linzer tart, 200–201
Liver, calf's, with port wine and
 ginger, 90
Lobster:
 or crayfish bisque, 50–51
 or crayfish stock, 52–53
 and vegetable broth, 51
Lop cheung (Chinese sausage), 233

M

Madeira sauce, warm confit of duck
 with, 102
Main courses, *see* Entrees
Marinated:
 beef short ribs, 73
 mushrooms, 185
 rib-eye with Gorgonzola sauce, 76
 scallops and watercress salad, 19
 skirt steak with horseradish
  mustard, 75
 tuna with spiced sprouts, 13
Mashed potatoes, 155
Mayonnaise, 179
 dill, gravlax with, 16–17
 and horseradish and mustard,
  178
Meat:
 barbecued baby back ribs, 86–87
 beef brisket, 77
 beef carpaccio, 14
 beef stroganoff, 78
 braised lamb steaks with oregano
  and feta, 84

calf's liver with port wine and
 ginger, 90
Chinese sausage salad, 9
grilled pepper steak with
 tamarind chutney, 74
grilled veal chops with thyme
 vinaigrette, 88
herb-stuffed leg of lamb with
 pimento sauce, 79–80
hot brisket of beef sandwiches,
 63
lamb curry with fried onions, 85–
 86
lamb's tongue with thyme
 vinaigrette, 18
lamb with sautéed eggplant and
 onion marmalade on naan, 61
marinated beef short ribs, 73
marinated rib-eye with
 Gorgonzola sauce, 76
marinated skirt steak with
 horseradish mustard, 75
moussaka, 81–83
roasted pork with two cabbages,
 62
Scotch eggs, 126
skirt steak on rye bread, 62
veal kidneys with lemon and soy,
 89
Melon salad, Thai, 8
Mint and cilantro chutney, 5
Mirin, 234
Mocha, iced, 230
Monkfish, roasted with coulis of
 turnips, 111–112
Moussaka, 81–83
Mushroom(s):
 chanterelle risotto, 120
 cream of, soup, 32
 marinated, 185
Mussel:
 bisque, 53–54
 and cockle stew, Portuguese, 116
Mustard:
 grilled swordfish with chopped
  shallots and, 106